CONDUCTING
FOCUS GROUPS

for BUSINESS *and* MANAGEMENT STUDENTS

WITHDRAWN

CONDUCTING FOCUS GROUPS

for BUSINESS and MANAGEMENT STUDENTS

CAROLINE OATES &
PANAYIOTA J. ALEVIZOU

Los Angeles | London | New Delhi
Singapore | Washington DC | Melbourne

Los Angeles | London | New Delhi
Singapore | Washington DC | Melbourne

SAGE Publications Ltd
1 Oliver's Yard
55 City Road
London EC1Y 1SP

SAGE Publications Inc.
2455 Teller Road
Thousand Oaks, California 91320

SAGE Publications India Pvt Ltd
B 1/I 1 Mohan Cooperative Industrial Area
Mathura Road
New Delhi 110 044

SAGE Publications Asia-Pacific Pte Ltd
3 Church Street
#10-04 Samsung Hub
Singapore 049483

Editor: Kirsty Smy
Assistant editor: Lyndsay Aitken
Production editor: Sarah Cooke
Copyeditor: William Baginsky
Proofreader: Thea Watson
Indexer: Judith Lavender
Marketing manager: Alison Borg
Cover design: Francis Kenney
Typeset by: C&M Digitals (P) Ltd, Chennai, India
Printed in the UK

Library of Congress Control Number: 2017938616

British Library Cataloguing in Publication data

A catalogue record for this book is available from
the British Library

ISBN 978-1-47394-821-1
ISBN 978-1-47394-822-8 (pbk)

At SAGE we take sustainability seriously. Most of our products are printed in the UK using FSC papers and boards.
When we print overseas we ensure sustainable papers are used as measured by the PREPS grading system.
We undertake an annual audit to monitor our sustainability.

CONTENTS

EDITORS' INTRODUCTION TO THE *MASTERING BUSINESS RESEARCH METHODS* SERIES

Welcome to the *Mastering Business Research Methods* series. In recent years, there has been a great increase in the numbers of students reading masters level degrees across the business and management disciplines. A great number of these students have to prepare a dissertation towards the end of their degree programme in a time-frame of three to four months. For many students, this takes place after their taught modules have finished and is expected to be an independent piece of work. Whilst each student is supported in their dissertation or research project by an academic supervisor, the student will need to find out more detailed information about the method that he or she intends to use. Before starting their dissertations or research projects these students have usually been provided with little more than an over-view across a wide range of methods as preparation for this often daunting task. If you are one such student, you are not alone. As university professors with a deep interest in research methods, we have provided this series of books to help students like you. Each book provides detailed information about a particular method to sup-port you in your dissertation. We understand both what is involved in masters level dissertations, and what help students need with regard to methods in order to excel when writing a dissertation. This series is the only one that is designed with the specific objective of helping masters level students to undertake and prepare their dissertations.

Each book in our series is designed to provide sufficient knowledge about either a method of data collection or a method of data analysis, and each book is intended to be read by the student when undertaking particular stages of the research pro-cess, such as data collection or analysis. Each book is written in a clear way by highly respected authors who have considerable experience of teaching and writing about research methods. To help students find their way around each book, we have utilised a standard format, with each book organised into six chapters:

- **Chapter 1** introduces the method, considers how the method emerged for what purposes, and provides an outline of the remainder of the book.
- **Chapter 2** addresses the underlying philosophical assumptions that inform the uses of particular methods.
- **Chapter 3** discusses the components of the relevant method.
- **Chapter 4** considers the way in which the different components may be organised to use the method.
- **Chapter 5** provides examples of published studies that have used the method.
- **Chapter 6** concludes by reflecting on the strengths and weaknesses of that method.

We hope that reading your chosen book helps you in your dissertation.

Bill Lee, Mark N.K. Saunders and V.K. Narayanan

ABOUT THE SERIES EDITORS

Bill Lee, PhD, is Professor of Accounting and Head of the Accounting and Financial Management Division at the University of Sheffield, UK. He has a long-standing interest in research methods and practice, in addition to his research into accounting and accountability issues. Bill's research has been published widely, including in: *Accounting Forum*; *British Accounting Review*; *Critical Perspectives on Accounting*; *Management Accounting Research*; *Omega*; and *Work, Employment & Society*. His publications in the area of research methods and practice include the co-edited collections *The Real Life Guide to Accounting Research* and *Challenges and Controversies in Management Research*.

Mark N.K. Saunders, BA MSc PGCE PhD FCIPD, is Professor of Business Research Methods at Birmingham Business School, University of Birmingham, UK. His research interests are research methods, in particular methods for understanding intra organisational relationships; human resource aspects of the management of change, in particular trust within and between organisations; and small and medium-sized enterprises. Mark's research has been published in journals including *Journal of Small Business Management*, *Field Methods*, *Human Relations*, *Management Learning* and *Social Science and Medicine*. He has co-authored and co-edited a range of books including *Research Methods for Business Students* (currently in its sixth edition) and the *Handbook of Research Methods on Trust*.

V.K. Narayanan is the Associate Dean for Research, Director of the Center for Research Excellence, and the Deloitte Touché Stubbs Professor of Strategy and Entrepreneurship in Drexel University, Philadelphia, PA. His articles have appeared in leading professional journals such as *Academy of Management Journal*, *Academy of Management Review*, *Accounting Organizations and Society*, *Journal of Applied Psychology*, *Journal of Management*, *Journal of Management Studies*, *Management Information Systems Quarterly*, *R&D Management* and *Strategic Management Journal*. Narayanan holds a bachelor's degree in mechanical engineering from the Indian Institute of Technology, Madras, a post graduate degree in business administration from the Indian Institute of Management, Ahmedabad, and a PhD in business from the Graduate School of Business at the University of Pittsburgh, Pennsylvania.

ABOUT THE AUTHORS

Caroline J. Oates has been researching and teaching qualitative methods in the marketing field for many years. Her first publication on research methods was a chapter on the use of focus groups, in *Research Training for Social Scientists: A Handbook for Postgraduate Researchers*, published by Sage. Since then, her numerous publications in marketing have drawn upon a range of qualitative methods including focus groups with both adults and children. Caroline is a full member of the Chartered Institute of Marketing, and the Academy of Marketing, where she set up the Special Interest Group in Sustainability Marketing. Caroline was the founder of the Centre for Research in Marketing and Society, located in the University of Sheffield Management School, where she currently works as senior lecturer.

Panayiota J. Alevizou is a lecturer in marketing in the University of Sheffield and an experienced marketing practitioner. She has used focus groups as a main research method for most of her publications. As a practitioner Panayiota organised and moderated focus groups for many years and in different European cities for consultancy projects. Panayiota leads an ongoing project, utilising focus groups, which evaluates on-pack sustainability claims for companies. She is an affiliated member of the Chartered Institute of Marketing and a member of the Centre for Research in Marketing and Society based in the Management School.

ACKNOWLEDGEMENTS

Our thanks go to all the students and colleagues, in academia and in practice, with whom we have had the pleasure of discussing qualitative research over many years. In particular, we extend our gratitude to Seonaidh, who has been our friend, colleague and mentor since the beginning. We also thank John, who generously offered many practitioner insights into using focus groups in market research.

Patience and encouragement, as ever, from Mark and Thomas.

Many thanks to my daughter Maria, who has supported me in every step.

1

INTRODUCTION

INTRODUCTION

Focus groups can be defined as 'group discussions organised to explore a specific set of issues' with 'the explicit use of the *group interaction* as research data' (Kitzinger, 1994: 103). Put more simply, they are sites of 'collective conversations' (Liamputtong, 2011). The focus group is a much-used technique in business and management research as it has the potential to produce rich, in-depth insights into a phenomenon and has a degree of flexibility in how it is structured for different research purposes. The focus group is more than a group interview (a term with which it is often used interchangeably; see below) and different to the notion of an individual interview, although there are some similarities. Focus groups can stand alone in a research project, or they can be combined with other methods, but they are almost always used to generate qualitative rather than quantitative data. A key element of the focus group in whatever research context it might be used, is the facilitation of interaction between participants. This feature sets the focus group apart from similar methods and makes it both extremely attractive as a means of gathering data, and at the same time rather challenging for someone conducting a focus group for the first time.

In this book, we aim to provide an accessible guide for the reader who wants to conduct focus groups as part of a business or management research project. While the book is written with masters-level students in mind, it is also likely to be useful for more experienced researchers who are undertaking their first focus group. In this introductory chapter, we place the focus group in its historical context, explaining how it emerged in the 20th century and how it has developed since then in the business and management disciplines. We look at some examples of how focus groups have been used in this academic context; introduce the kinds of data that might be generated by focus groups; and then outline the remaining five chapters of this book.

HISTORY OF THE FOCUS GROUP

It is widely accepted that focus groups have been used by market researchers since the 1920s (Basch, 1987) and that early use of group interviews has been documented in social science research from around the same time. Even so, focus groups were traditionally viewed as more of a practitioner technique than one suitable for academic purposes. Focus groups gradually came to be incorporated more in academic research from the 1940s, when Merton used what he called 'focused interviews' in the context of investigating persuasive communications in the US during the Second World War (Merton et al., 1956). The existing quantitative research approach involved groups of participants simply and individually recording their positive/negative reactions to material. Merton developed this into an increasingly nuanced set of procedures which allowed group participants to express their subjective reactions (Bloor et al., 2001). These procedures formed the basis of early academic writings on focus groups by Merton and his colleagues (Merton et al., 1956) and remain at the core of focus group research as we know it today.

Focus groups tended to remain largely in the marketing and public relations spheres, and even now many people automatically associate focus groups with this kind of marketing research, for example bringing consumers together to discuss a new product launch, or to comment on a current advertising campaign. Such focus groups in this commercial context are usually organised by market research agencies, which have many resources at their disposal that include incentives to offer participants, purpose-built locations, sophisticated recording equipment and so on. These applications are intended to produce data that would not be appropriate for more academic research. These practitioner focus groups can be characterised by their standardised format with specific questions generated by the client and posed by a professional moderator who conducts the group. The moderator leads the discussion, maintaining the conversation and gathering responses from all the participants. Hence, there is likely to be more interaction between the moderator and the participants than between the participants themselves. This approach is completely acceptable in a commercial context, and fulfils its purpose. For academic research the expectation would be for the moderator to encourage and facilitate interaction between the participants, rather than between her/himself and the participants, often with the intention of investigating meanings and interpretations. Here, the moderation is likely to be performed by the researcher him/herself, rather than using a professional moderator. As we show in Chapter 2, focus groups can be organised in a number of ways according to purpose, so there is scope for various degrees of structure. In this book we discuss the different formats of focus groups as appropriate to an academic research project. We also explain the moderator role in further detail in Chapter 4.

Although focus groups are often associated with marketing research, they have actually been adopted in most research fields. Stewart and Shamdasani (2015) identify the many disciplines that have embraced focus groups over the decades, and we include the ones that are relevant to the topic of this book: organisation behaviour, information systems, communications, management, and marketing. In some areas of management, focus groups have not been used so widely, for example in logistics, but there is a call for more use of this method in what has been a traditionally quantitative field of research (Rodrigues et al., 2010). Today, focus groups are used extensively in social sciences research: a brief search of the first issue of 2016 of *Qualitative Market Research: An International Journal* demonstrates that out of six research papers that were published, two were based on using focus groups. These include a study by Knittel et al. (2016) into brand avoidance by Generation Y consumers, which takes a multi-methods approach, combining focus groups with individual interviews. We look at this study in more detail in Chapter 5. The second article is by Gadalla et al. (2016) and is concerned with a new area of focus group research, that of avatars in the virtual environment of Second Life. Here, the relative merits of traditional face-to-face focus groups, online focus groups, and those based on avatars, are compared and contrasted.

DIFFERENCES BETWEEN FOCUS GROUPS AND GROUP INTERVIEWS

The terms 'focus group' and 'group interview' are sometimes used interchangeably to mean the same technique. It is useful to consider what makes the two different, as on the surface they do seem very similar. See Table 1.1.

Table 1.1 Focus groups and group interviews

	Rationale	*Interaction*	*Data*	*Depth*
Focus groups	Designed to facilitate interaction	Between participants	Group discussion and debate	Topic is explored in depth
Group interviews	Quicker way to interview than using individual techniques	Between moderator and participants	Individual responses	Topic ranges widely

These distinctions are not always clear cut but focus groups will often be part of a qualitative research design, where the aim is to study how people collectively understand and make sense of phenomena. A further comparison can be made between focus groups that are created specifically for research purposes, and groups that occur naturally. This is particularly pertinent in organisation studies, where it is possible to design research which can use either method. Steyaert and Bouwen (2004) recount how they used both methods in a study of innovation in SMEs. They offer a useful example which directly compares the two methods which they term group interview (i.e. a specifically created focus group) and project group (i.e. a group that already exists as part of the organisational environment). These 'created' and 'natural' group forms can be distinguished in terms of research goal, methodological focus, data generation and analysis, and the roles of the group and the researcher. For example, the researcher in a created focus group context acts as a moderator, which means they facilitate the group discussion. In a natural group setting, they would be more like an observing participant. Steyaert and Bouwen (2004) stress that the distinction between these two kinds of groups is not discrete, and should be viewed on a continuum according to the influence of the researcher on the group situation.

TYPES OF DATA COLLECTED

So far, we have emphasised the potential of focus groups to provide qualitative data although we have also noted that in some situations they might be used to generate a more structured response which could lend itself to quantitative analysis. For example, it would be possible to ask group participants to record their reactions to a proposed new kerbside recycling scheme using a 1–5 Likert scale for measures including convenience, transparency, propensity to recycle and so on. This approach would produce quantifiable data (i.e. data that is collected in numerical form) with potential for statistical analysis. It would conform to the underlying philosophical assumptions of positivism, with the aim of collecting objective data in a replicable study. The interaction between participants would be minimal in such a research design, making it more like a group interview than a focus group, although there would be an opportunity for more qualitative techniques to be used as well, depending on the question that the researcher is attempting to answer.

However, for the purpose of a masters-level research project, consideration of focus groups would more likely be rooted in a desire for rich, in-depth qualitative data. By this, we mean data that is not viewed in numerical terms, but is consistent with meanings, interpretations, how participants make sense of things and how they articulate this to the other participants. In other words, *why* they think as they do. Focus groups, when moderated sensitively and with skill, excel at producing this kind of data. With a fairly open protocol or discussion guide/agenda (list of themes/key words/overall questions/activities) a moderator can present the topic to be discussed with the necessary flexibility and agility to pursue unexpected avenues of thought, or to pick up emerging themes as they develop during the group session. Merton et al. (1956) called this 'range', by which they meant the extent of relevant data provided by the focus group, including aspects which were not anticipated. These aspects can, if considered important and relevant to the topic, be incorporated in the protocol for the next focus group. In this way, each focus group might add something different to the previous one, even though the central topic is the same. We illustrate the notion of range in Box 1.1.

Box 1.1   Range in focus group research

As part of a wider research project on the consumption of popular culture in the UK, Oates (2000) decided to take a qualitative approach to investigate how readers of best-selling women's magazines consumed these particular titles. Previous research had established that readers used the magazines as sources of entertainment and information, but this practical use did not explain the loyalty and affection in which the magazines were held. Oates used her personal networks to arrange focus groups with a range of readers in different settings, such as financial institutions, libraries and churches, with the aim of investigating whether the social context of consumption (i.e. the environment in which the magazines were acquired, read, and shared) could be relevant to the magazines' success. Themes that began to emerge from the initial data collection and analysis suggested the magazines were central to notions of family and friendship networks, integral to building and maintaining relationships between women. This insight allowed the research to move into an unexpectedly rich and related area – that of gift giving. Thus, the extent or range of data produced a hitherto unanticipated direction to the project.

The example in Box 1.1 illustrates the value of carrying out data collection and data analysis concurrently, rather than gathering all the data at once, and then beginning the process of analysis. Reflecting on each focus group as it happens offers the space to incorporate new insights into subsequent groups. Another example of how using focus groups can move research into related but unexpected discoveries comes from an international project on labelling, and is presented in Box 1.2.

Box 1.2   Range in focus group research in an international context

Alevizou et al. (2015) investigated the process of encoding and decoding eco-labels on a range of household products such as food and cosmetics. Their aim was to understand how consumers interpret the many varieties of label. Carrying out initial

(Continued)

(Continued)

focus groups in Greece and the UK, two European countries with very different experiences of sustainability, they started with a basic protocol which involved showing examples of on-pack labels to shoppers to gather impressions about the labels, and what meanings they had for shoppers. This approach produced much confusion in the focus groups, as participants did not recognise or understand what the labels were intended to signify. What began to emerge was the importance of different kinds of knowledge that participants drew upon to make sense of their (in)comprehension, and it was this diversion into multiple levels of knowledge that became part of the data collection. It became clear that the focus of the research inquiry should progress from looking at recognition and decoding, to probing sources of knowledge. Thus, Alevizou et al. (2015) developed the protocol for subsequent focus groups to include questions designed to elicit information about which knowledge base the participants were using to make sense of the many labels.

The potential for flexibility in focus groups is one of their advantages, as we have illustrated with these two examples from our own research. To be confident enough to work with such a degree of flexibility demands practice, but as shown above, it can lead to (sometimes unanticipated) rich sets of qualitative data. For example, Ahrens (2004) recounts how he was able to carry out research in a bank, investigating integrated performance measurement, including two group interviews which, although not labelled as focus groups, demonstrated characteristics typical of this method. The first interview he admitted was 'boring' yet it led to unexpected insights into the management accounting department of the bank. The second one led to an opportunity to shadow one of the managers for three days.

THE ROLE OF THE FOCUS GROUP IN DIFFERENT RESEARCH DESIGNS

In Chapter 2, we look at the various purposes that focus groups can be used for according to the research approach taken, which is underpinned by considerations of ontology and epistemology. Before that, we finish this chapter by discussing how focus groups can be part of a research design in three different ways – as a stand-alone method; as part of a multi-methods design with additional qualitative methods; and in combination with quantitative methods in a mixed methods design. Which design is chosen will depend on the research question to be answered. We illustrate each design with an example of a typical masters research project from business and management studies, starting with Box 1.3 where we provide an example of using focus groups as the only method in a masters dissertation. The choice to collect all your data from focus groups only would need to be carefully considered, but it is perfectly possible to generate a set of appropriately in-depth data to answer a research question in this way.

Box 1.3   Using focus groups as a stand-alone method design

Zaiqing is studying for a masters in Consumer Behaviour. She is very interested in the roles of trust and emotion in consumer decision making and has decided to research how parents in China purchase vitamin and mineral supplements for their children. From her own experience she is aware that this is an issue that causes anxiety in parents, as there have been cases of fraudulent products on the market which can be detrimental to children's wellbeing. From her review of the literature on decision making, Zaiqing sees that little work has been done at a family level on how such products are researched and purchased, but she feels the family context might be important. Thus, she decides to use focus groups with extended families to look at trust and emotion in this particular purchasing context. With the use of a protocol including questions based on consumer behaviour theory about the decision making process, she conducts two initial family focus groups as the pilot for her masters dissertation project. On analysing her data, she realises that the family context is regarded as less influential on decision making than that of friendship and informal network groups with other mothers, who are the primary decision makers. Thus, in her next set of focus groups she also asks participants to discuss other influencers in this context. Zaiqing conducts six focus groups in total as the basis for her dissertation.

Using focus groups in a multi-methods design

Focus groups have the flexibility to be used in a second approach which is the multi-methods design. Here, additional qualitative methods such as interviews, participant observation, and/or diary keeping are used alongside the focus groups. For example, a study by Horta et al. (2013) investigating food consumption used documentary analysis, visual analysis, direct observation, interviews with several stakeholders, as well as focus groups with parents and children. The purpose of taking such an approach is to benefit from the various insights that the different data can provide, all centred on the phenomenon under study. Sometimes, this might be characterised as a case study (Bryman, 2016), as case study design will involve more than one method. In Box 1.4 we provide an example of how focus groups might be used in a multi-methods design.

Box 1.4 Using focus groups as part of a multi-methods design

Priya has decided to research the market potential for organic produce amongst teenage consumers in the Indian market for her MBA dissertation. From her literature review, she has discovered that there is actually little research in this specific area and what there is has been carried out in a quantitative way, using surveys. She thinks that taking a qualitative approach would add to existing knowledge by surfacing consumer (mis)understandings of the term organic in an Indian context. Priya decides that focus groups with teenagers would be the best way to address her research aims but she is also aware that although teenagers might be the consumers of products, they do not necessarily purchase them. She therefore decides to combine the focus groups with individual interviews with parents of the teenagers to ask them about purchase requests and general shopping and consumption habits. For the focus groups, Priya decides to start with open questions, letting the participants discuss and then offer what they understand the term organic to mean. She then shares a pre-prepared set of cards featuring various terms to do with organic (e.g. no pesticides, additive-free, non-chemical) for the teenagers to discuss and sort, so she can observe both what they do (not) understand, and what is (un)important to them. Priya is also interested in the possibility of peer influence in the decision to adopt/reject organic products so she has some questions around the kind of person who would/would not purchase organic products. With this multi-methods research design, Priya thinks that she will be able to gather enough data to provide insights into how teenagers understand and consider organic products from the focus groups, and their actual behaviour in consuming such products from the interviews.

Using focus groups in a mixed methods design

It is common to find focus groups used in a mixed methods design in masters research projects. This design means that a combination of qualitative and quantitative methods is used in the same research project. Often, focus groups are employed after some data has been collected by other means, for example as a way of aiding interpretation of quantitative findings from a survey. In a more practical sense, a quantitative survey could help to identify participants who are willing to take part in a later focus group. Alternatively, focus groups may be used at the beginning of data collection to inform the design of subsequent methods such as a questionnaire. Easterby-Smith et al. (2015) acknowledge that mixed methods are increasingly used in research with organisations because such an approach can provide several perspectives on what is being studied. However, they also sound a note of caution, in that the researcher should be careful when using mixed methods as they can lead to contradictory results. We illustrate the use of focus groups in such a design in Box 1.5.

Box 1.5   Using focus groups as part of a mixed methods design

Alex is studying for a masters in Entrepreneurship and wants to find out how owner-managers of new micro-organisations use networks to help them set up and develop their businesses. From his course so far, he knows that networks can be a key part of organisational success but he wants to find out why some micro-organisations seem to be more successful than others at networking. Alex wants to use his findings to make a difference to the local business community and he needs a research design that will allow him to gather enough data to make generalisations. However, he isn't sure what he needs to ask to enable him to answer his research question. He thinks it might be something to do with the owner-managers themselves so he decides to start his research with an exploratory focus group comprising seven owner-managers of local micro-organisations. He therefore begins by asking participants to talk about themselves and how they set up their businesses. He then follows up with questions about the role of networks in this process – for example, how owners might know about networks, whether they get involved, and what might be the barriers and facilitators to participation. This data elicitation provides a wealth of information which, on examination, emphasises the importance of external factors such as industry sector and location of business, and internal factors to do with the owners' willingness to embrace new ideas and opportunities. Alex then uses the insights from this focus group to inform the design of an online questionnaire which incorporates sections covering external factors and a psychological scale for personality to address internal factors. This enables him to collect enough quantitative data to test the relationship between networking and the other variables.

When combining focus groups with other methods in a mixed methods design, it is helpful to consider which method is dominating the research inquiry. Morgan (1996) offers a useful way of looking at this and suggests four ways of thinking about how to combine focus groups with surveys:

1. Surveys act as the primary method and focus groups serve in a preliminary capacity. This would be a common use of focus groups, where they help to inform the design of a questionnaire for example.

2. Surveys are again seen as the primary method, but the focus group now acts as a follow-up that assists in interpreting the survey results, especially where there may be some poorly understood results that merit further clarification.
3. Focus groups are the primary method while surveys provide preliminary inputs that guide their application. Here, researchers might use the quantitative data from surveys to select samples for focus groups or topics for more detailed analysis.
4. Focus groups again act as the primary method and surveys are used as a source of follow-up data, although this combination is not such a commonly used research design.

INDIVIDUAL INTERVIEWS

We mentioned in an earlier example that individual interviews can be used as part of a research design involving focus groups, thus indicating that the two methods can bring something different but related to the research. Interviews with one individual can take various forms, depending on the degree of structure and the purpose of the interview. For example, Cassell (2015) identifies ten types of interview, ranging from a structured design aimed at information gathering which can produce quantifiable data to an unstructured design based on phenomenology which generates insights into an individual's lifeworld. It is also possible to interview more than one individual at the same time in what is known as a dyad (two) or triad (three) interview. These might be seen as very small focus groups if the purpose is to generate interaction between the participants, or might be treated more like a group interview, where the emphasis is on answering questions posed by the moderator/interviewer. Often with dyads and triads, the participants will already know each other, for example parent and child, or co-workers. They are commonly used in market research but can also be found in academic studies, although sometimes the dyad participants are actually interviewed separately (e.g. Gentina and Singh's (2015) study using mother/adolescent dyads). Small focus groups are thought to be suitable for use with particular populations, such as children, as they are less intimidating than larger groups. For example, in a study of adolescent impulse buyers, Brici et al. (2013) deliberately chose to limit their group size to three or four participants, as they acknowledged that teenagers can be shy. Generally, the line is rather blurred when it comes to defining interviews that include more than one person, as depending on the research purpose they could be treated as paired interviews or as mini focus groups. Typically, a focus group would involve between four and twelve participants, although from our experience we would suggest that eight is a more manageable maximum number. Twelve would be a large group to manage, even for an experienced moderator. We look at group composition and moderation in further detail in Chapters 3 and 4.

APPROACH TAKEN WITHIN THIS BOOK

This introductory chapter has set the scene for using focus groups in a dissertation or project, and has briefly illustrated the potential of focus groups. To help you negotiate your way through the challenges and issues of planning a research study using this method, we discuss in Chapter 2 the philosophical underpinnings to research, and outline the various purposes that focus groups can fulfil, illustrated with examples from typical masters projects in business and management. Chapter 2 thus provides the context which helps the reader to make an informed decision about whether to use this method for their own research project before reading the next chapters. In Chapter 3, we look at the basic components of focus groups, including consideration of how to choose the focus group format, developing the discussion agenda, and the importance of planning and designing focus groups. In Chapter 4, we look at the focus group itself, the role of the moderator, and debate the practicalities of actually moderating (conducting) a focus group, together with ethical considerations. We also look at what happens after a group has finished. In Chapter 5, further examples of how focus groups have been used in the business and management literature are provided, and in Chapter 6, the advantages and disadvantages of using focus groups are summarised, and there are suggestions for the next steps in using focus groups.

The overall aim of this book is to provide an accessible and readable guide to using focus groups as part of a masters dissertation or project in business and management studies. We present both the opportunities to be gained from using focus groups, but also the challenges inherent in this method. Conducting focus groups can be a very rewarding experience but we acknowledge it can also be difficult, especially at the start. Like all research, it is helpful to be prepared, and we hope this book goes some way to aiding that preparation as part of your positive research experience.

2

UNDERSTANDING FOCUS GROUPS

INTRODUCTION

The aim of this chapter is to introduce the reader to the different types of focus groups that can be used in business and management research and to provide an overview of the purpose that such focus groups can address. In this chapter, we document the extent to which focus groups are compatible with different epistemological and ontological traditions so that you can assess whether the philosophical standpoint adopted and the arguments to be developed are consistent with the types of data to be used. First, we discuss how considerations of philosophical approach will influence the researcher's choice of focus group. We present the different structures of focus groups with examples from student projects. We then consider what criteria should be taken into account when assessing the quality of a research inquiry.

UNDERSTANDING FOCUS GROUP VARIATIONS

A researcher new to the idea of conducting a focus group might be unaware that such a method of collecting data can take different forms. Without reflection, the focus group might simply be seen as a quicker way to gather data rather than interviewing each participant individually (Ghauri and Grønhaug, 2005). However, careful consideration of focus groups will be underpinned by the epistemological understanding of the researcher, which in turn will affect how the focus group is imagined and structured. There is no single correct way to design a focus group but there are several preliminary decisions to be made to ensure that the method is in alignment with the overall research project.

PHILOSOPHICAL APPROACH

As indicated above, both the choice of focus groups as a method for collecting data, and how they might look in action, are guided by philosophical assumptions. Saunders et al. (2016: 124) define research philosophy as 'a system of beliefs and assumptions about the development of knowledge'. Generally, focus groups are associated with a qualitative and inductive approach, with few participants, and favoured by researchers working within a broadly defined interpretive worldview. This does not necessarily preclude their use within other philosophical assumptions. For example, those working with a positivist understanding of epistemology might attempt to use focus groups to generate objective data, although this would resemble a structured group interview rather more than a focus group. We define philosophical assumptions below.

Defining philosophical assumptions

Ontology can be defined as the study of being and social reality, and is rooted in the Greek word *on* which means 'being' or 'that which is' and *logos*, which translates as the study, or science, of something. The fundamental questions researchers ask about ontology are, 'What can be said to exist, and is there just one or are there multiple realities?'. The underlying assumptions of a researcher adopting a realist ontology include a belief that what is being studied exists independently as an external reality. A world distinct from the researcher is present and can be discovered. On the other hand, taking a constructionist view of reality indicates that the researcher believes that reality is not objective and exterior; rather it is given meaning by people, including researchers themselves, and there is no single reality. Here, the phenomena under study are created through the interactions and discourse of social actors.

Epistemology means the study of the nature of knowledge: how we know what is knowledge, what is considered acceptable knowledge, how it is acquired, and how best to go about the process of inquiry. The term comes from the Greek word *episteme*, which means 'knowledge'. It is important for undertaking any kind of project that researchers ask themselves what kind of knowledge they think can be generated through their research. In general, there are two broad approaches to knowledge. First, an objective or positivistic approach in which the researcher adopts the view of the natural sciences, which in turn leads to generalisations and quantifiable observations, appropriate for statistical analysis. Positivists believe that it is possible directly to study and understand reality. The researcher seeks to find causal relationships, and is careful to remain at a distance from the research process. The second approach is subjective, where the researcher prioritises understanding over causal explanation, privileging sense-making and meaning. From this perspective, the management researcher does not accept that there is a single ready-made world available out there for discovery, but attempts to understand the process of symbolic world-making. Here, the

researcher does not occupy a position of neutral observer, but reports their own interpretation within the understanding that everyone sees the world differently. Another
way of expressing the difference is the contrast between defining the world as it is or
the world as perceived (Moses and Knutsen, 2012).

It follows from the above description that focus groups fit best within the underlying
assumptions around a subjectivist epistemology, which in turn tend to lead to a qualitative methodology. However, as we discussed in Chapter 1, focus groups can also be part
of a mixed methods design, for example as a precursor to a questionnaire. On their own,
focus groups are not seen as staples of quantitative research – they do not offer the
opportunity for large samples, or generalisability, nor do they readily lend themselves
to statistical analysis. In common with other qualitative methods such as unstructured
interviews, focus groups have the ability to provide insights into process rather than
outcome (Barbour, 2007). A frequently cited quote from Morgan sums up this valuable aspect: 'focus groups are useful when it comes to investigating *what* participants
think, but they excel at uncovering *why* participants think as they do' (1988: 25). Such
insight is possible because of the interactive nature of focus groups, which privilege the
interaction generated as members of the group articulate, explain and challenge each
other. Participants expose the reasoning behind their own opinions, allowing the moderator to explore and record such interaction. For example, a focus group with employees
attempting to find out what kind of infrastructure would encourage more recycling at
work might reveal a consensus on what the bins should look like, but further probing
might yield data that underlay that group assessment. In this case, it might be that
the normative understandings drawn upon by group members reveal a common perception that recyclables end up in mainstream rubbish further down the line anyway,
so the organisation's attempt to increase recycling is just another waste of employee
time. Thus a focus group which is positioned to generate quite surface-level information
on the design of recycling receptacles could actually offer much more in-depth understanding of the norms underlying employee behaviour, which are rarely articulated.
As Bloor et al. (2001: 4) note, the access that focus groups provide to group meanings,
processes and norms is the reason why they are so popular in academic research.

However, these unique features of focus groups are not without problems and they
can be challenging for all researchers. This is because participants may not be consistent, and may display frequent changes of opinion as they listen and respond to the
views of others. Of course, this is totally interesting and absorbing from a research
perspective if the researcher is gathering data on how people think about a topic and
form their attitudes, like in the employee recycling example earlier, but is not helpful
if one is attempting to pin down attitudes as fixed or permanent. What participants
articulate within a focus group is exactly that – it is context-bound and responsive to an
initial agenda set by the moderator, then shaped and affected by the other participants.

In addition, any researcher expecting a clear 'group view' to emerge at the con-
clusion of the discussion may well be disappointed. Each focus group is made up of

individuals and whilst there may or may not be a general consensus, it is important to take into account the interchanges between participants, rather than hoping for a united front. To have this expectation in mind would not enable full advantage to be taken of the focus group's interactive features. Further, the researcher might take note of emerging differences between participants, perhaps based on demographics or experiences, which can usefully lead to further questions or subsequent focus groups or other research methods. In Box 2.1, we offer an example of how philosophical assumptions might underpin a student research project.

Box 2.1 Understanding your epistemological approach

Annie is studying for a masters degree in Management and for her dissertation she is delighted that she has negotiated access to several firms that operate in the same industrial sector. Building on her first degree in Operations Management, she wants to know how these firms combine their performance management systems with sustainability reporting. Like many students, she has been introduced to ontology and epistemology for the first time in her research methods module and is beginning to work through the debates to find her own position as a researcher. She starts from a realist ontology and has an expectation that she will find the answer to her research question. Having conducted a pilot focus group, she realises that there is no single answer to her question and that there may be multiple realities at play here. She therefore shifts to a constructionist ontology to enable a range of voices and opinions to come through in her findings. By conducting focus groups with the managers in these different firms, Annie is able to access their subjective interpretations of these specific management practices and understand how and why they are implemented in different ways.

Having outlined these philosophical positions, it is probably fair to say that in practice, the differences between them are not always so marked. There is often some blurring of boundaries, not so much in the actual underlying beliefs about the different ontologies and epistemologies, as these are basically distinct, but in the choice of methods used in a particular research design. What can happen with focus groups is that they may actually operate more like structured group interviews if the underlying philosophical assumption is based on a realist ontology and objective epistemology (i.e. there is an observable exterior world which can be measured and in turn produce quantitative data, leading to law-like generalisations). For example, a researcher adopting a realist ontology and objective epistemology might use a focus group to surface opinions and attitudes in a factual way, often as a precursor to a quantitative study. Like a structured individual interview, a group interview will make use of a fixed protocol (i.e. a set of questions, asked in the same order), thereby providing consistency across the data collection, and perhaps assigning numerical values to the resulting data. Coule (2013) offers an insightful methodological critique of how focus groups have been used by researchers who accept the deployment of qualitative data collection methods whilst retaining key characteristics of positivism. She emphasises that how the focus group is positioned in relation to theories of knowledge will inform its aims, characteristics, analysis and role of reflexivity. By being explicit about one's epistemological position, the role of the focus group in producing a particular kind of knowledge will also be clear. Such transparency will ensure that a focus group method is not adopted unthinkingly, but used with critical reflection on the knowledge generated. For example, as a contrast to the focus group informed by realist/objectivist assumptions which produces objective data, a focus group designed from an interpretive stance would aim to access intersubjective meanings and produce rich, complex data in an attempt to account for behaviour in everyday contexts and situations.

Thus, the reasons for using focus groups within a specific research agenda will vary, but the emphasis can be on process as well as the actual outcome. Focus groups might be used at any stage of a research project (beginning, middle, end) in combination with other methods, or stand alone, depending on the purpose of the research (see Chapter 1). In Table 2.1 we identify the most frequently cited contexts for choosing focus groups that are applicable to business and management, and illustrate how these might look in a research project.

Table 2.1   Structure and purpose of focus groups

Level of structure	Type of focus group	Purpose of focus group
Unstructured	Exploratory	Introduce a new topic for research, or obtain general background information about a topic, or generate survey questions
Semi-structured	Theoretical	Generate data to inform theory development
Semi-structured	Impression gathering	Gather impressions of products, services, brands, organisations
Semi-structured	Diagnostic	Diagnose problems and/or success factors for a new product or service
Semi-structured	Explanatory	As an interpretive aid to examine survey findings

Developed from Stewart and Shamdasani, 2015: 44–45; Bloor et al., 2001: 17

DIFFERENT TYPES OF FOCUS GROUP STRUCTURE FOR DIFFERENT PURPOSES

As outlined in the previous section, focus groups can be structured in several ways according to purpose. We next consider the different structures aligned with the purpose of the focus group, starting with the unstructured format.

Unstructured focus groups

Unstructured focus groups tend to be led more by the participants than by the moderator, although there will be a topic guide, which may be as brief as an opening question or statement to set off the discussion. Such focus groups might be located within an interpretivist stance with the aim of accessing and understanding meanings, if the aim is to explore a new topic, guided by the participants themselves. An unstructured format could also be used to obtain data seen in a more objective way, for example by market researchers who want to gather opinions and attitudes in order to find out further information about a phenomenon.

Exploratory focus groups

For a research project which is intended to investigate a new topic, or a relatively under-explored area, the use of exploratory focus groups would be appropriate. For a new topic, perhaps where limited research has been done, the emphasis is very much on discovery. Hence, the research protocol, or list of questions or themes, would be fairly brief compared to focus groups for other research purposes. This is not to say there would be no guide at all for the moderator, but it would be minimal and open-ended to encourage as much discussion as possible by the participants. Indeed, the researcher might not know what to ask anyway and simply start with a basic question. Morgan and Scannell (1998: 45) offer an example which illustrates this rather elusive approach to focus groups. The research topic was aimed at understanding caregiving and nursing homes, and at the time very little was known about the transition of caring from home to an institutional setting, hence the choice of focus groups as the research method. There was a basic opening question to start each group ('When you think about your caregiving, what kinds of things make your life easier and what kinds of things make it harder?') which was sufficient to prompt a long and relevant discussion, without further intervention from the moderator. In this manner, the researchers learned a huge amount about this unique situation, expressed in the participants' own words, which allowed them to understand the stress inherent in the transition of caregiving. So a choice to use an exploratory focus group design would be based on the researcher being interested in learning what matters to the participants, what kind of language they use to discuss the topic and how they feel about it.

Another way of looking at exploratory focus groups is put forward by Bloor et al. (2001) who suggest that such focus groups be used in the early stages of a project to inform the later stages which might employ different methods (e.g. a survey). As with the example above, the situation would be one where relatively little is known about the topic, where prior research is lacking, to access the everyday language of the research participants or where the target group (e.g. adolescents) holds knowledge which is concealed from others. They make the point that if this research design is to be followed, sufficient time must be allowed to analyse the focus group data so it becomes meaningful to the remainder of the project. This combination of various methods would be an example of using a mixed methods design (see Chapter 1). An example of using exploratory focus groups from the consumer behaviour field is provided in Box 2.2.

Box 2.2   Designing an unstructured focus group for exploratory purposes using visual techniques

Marta is studying for a masters in Marketing with a specific focus on consumer behaviour. She is interested in how people make consumption decisions in their everyday social contexts and wants to focus on the under-explored consumer segment of teenage boys. Her research objective, which is informed by an interpretivist stance, is to explore perceptions around the influence of peers on boys' choice of clothing. She decides that exploratory focus groups would be a good way to investigate this objective, as very little is known about the topic. She realises that conducting research with teenagers is likely to be challenging, particularly in terms of ethics. She has completed a thorough ethics application and received written authorisation to participate in the research from schools, parents and the teenagers themselves. She is also uncertain about how to phrase questions, for example the appropriate language to use. As a way of overcoming this uncertainty, and to encourage the articulation of feelings in the focus groups, she plans to incorporate a simple comic strip scenario, as a form of completion technique (Malhotra, 2010). Completion techniques require participants to complete a partial situation. Marta plans to ask the boys to complete the second scene in a comic strip, using drawings and/or speech bubbles, to show how they would react to friends making fun of their chosen jacket. By utilising this approach, Marta will be able to access the boys' reactions to peer disapproval and use the comic strips as a focal point to prompt further discussions as they arise, for example around clothing for other purposes such as school and sport. She will use the focus group data to address her research objective of how boys perceive peer pressure and the influence of peers on consumption decisions.

Semi-structured focus groups

In academic research, most focus groups will come under this heading of semi-structured, although such a design can serve different purposes. Here, focus groups follow an outline of themes and questions to be delivered by the moderator but there remains flexibility to explore unanticipated themes or follow new trains of thought if they still relate to the original research design. Some researchers refer to this semi-structured approach as moderately structured groups (Morgan and Scannell, 1998) but still emphasise the need to match this design with the project's goals. It should not be seen as a default position for focus group design, or some kind of compromise, but needs to be clearly articulated within the project or dissertation.

Using semi-structured focus groups to generate data to inform theory development

The first use of focus groups within a semi-structured format is to generate data which will enable the development of theory. Here, the researcher is intending to design their focus groups to produce data which they will then analyse to make a contribution to a particular theory. Focus groups can be used as a single method here, or as part of a multi- or mixed methods design. The discussion guide will draw upon extant literature centred on a specific theory or theories and contain a number of questions and themes, but retain an openness which allows for emergent themes to be explored. An example of this focus group design is given in Box 2.3.

Box 2.3   Designing a semi-structured focus group to generate data to enable theory development

Helen is studying for a masters in Environmental Management and is keen to investigate how environmental tasks are performed in a household setting. Most research on behaviours such as recycling and energy reduction have been focused on the individual as the unit of analysis but Helen sees merit in situating such research at a household level, to reflect the context where many environmental behaviours are located. She has read widely around household decision making and has identified a gap in how this practice relates to recycling. Drawing upon the household decision making literature, Helen decides that interviewing all members of a household about how they perform recycling tasks will enable her to collect data to explore this phenomenon. Thus, she chooses focus groups as her only method and plans to carry out focus groups with different types of households (e.g. couple, family, shared, student). She aims to build a theory of how recycling is negotiated and performed between the members of different households, developing a conceptual framework in an inductive approach.

Using semi-structured focus groups to gather impressions

The next use we have classified under semi-structured focus groups is for the purpose of gathering impressions. Here, the aim of the focus group is to offer the researcher an understanding of how participants, usually in a defined target group, perceive something which might be novel to them, and this approach can be used across business and management research. For example, in human resource management researchers might use such a focus group to find out what employees think about potential policies or solution strategies (Krueger and Casey, 2015). Often with this semi-structured or moderately structured design, questions take a funnel format, in that questions move the discussion from a broad view, to a focus on three or four central topics, then finally to more specific and detailed concerns (Morgan and Scannell, 1998). We discuss structure and moderator role in more depth in Chapters 3 and 4. In Box 2.4 we offer an example from international business.

Box 2.4   Designing a semi-structured focus group for impression gathering

Ren is studying for a masters degree in International Business and wants to use his dissertation to explore the feasibility of launching a traditional Chinese dried food product which would be new to the UK mainstream market. In a multi-methods design, he has already arranged access to interview some grocery retailers to see if they would be interested in trialling the product. However, he feels that a focus group with a convenience sample of male and female food shoppers would contribute to his understanding of how the product might be accepted or not in a different culture, and therefore aid in answering his research objective of evaluating the market for this new product. Ren intends to ask shoppers at a local supermarket if they are the main preparer of household meals and, if so, whether they would be willing to participate in a focus group. He thinks that shoppers might possibly be confused about the food and how to prepare it, and how it might be incorporated into their usual repertoire of meals. Ren has prepared one or two broad introductory questions to start the focus group about favourite meals, food preparation and knowledge of dried products, with central questions to follow around usability, expectations, similarity and so on, and then several questions to cover specifics such as health properties, in case these do not arise naturally. He has also brought along samples of the dried product for participants to look at and handle. Ren is planning, with participants' permission, to audio record the focus group so that he can capture participants' initial vocal reactions to and impressions of the product as they encounter it for the first time, and he intends to note their facial expressions too as part of his data collection. This will enable him to consider any changes, for example to the packaging design or labelling information, as raised by the participants, which may influence the success of the product trial in a new market.

Using diagnostic semi-structured focus groups

The third kind of focus group we have included under a semi-structured design is that of the diagnostic focus group. As its name suggests, this focus group is intended to probe how a particular target audience responds to a new product or service, or a change in organisational structure or practice, particularly whether there are any problems or notable factors which account for its failure or success. A famous example from the marketing literature recounts how sales of a new product (boxed cake mix) failed to make an impact on the target market of housewives in America in the 1950s. Analysis of diagnostic focus group data revealed that women were not purchasing the product because they felt they should be putting more effort into cake making for their families than merely mixing pre-prepared powder with some water. The manufacturer removed the powdered egg from the box and replaced it with the instruction to 'add an egg'. This created the effect of actually making the cake more like baking from scratch and was therefore acceptable to the target market at the time (Morgan, 1998). We provide an example from a masters project in Box 2.5.

Box 2.5   Designing a semi-structured focus group to diagnose problems and/or success factors

Rani is interested in how large service organisations approach the development of their employees and as part of her masters in Human Resource Management project she wants to investigate the introduction of a new mentoring scheme in the global accountancy practice where she worked previously. Informally, she has heard mixed reports about the scheme from her old colleagues and thinks that there is scope for a research inquiry which will offer multiple perspectives of this phenomenon. Her approach to the research is informed by a constructionist ontology and a subjective epistemology, and she thinks that employees' interpretations of the scheme will be context dependent (e.g. be influenced by their position and status). Rani's objective in using diagnostic focus groups is to access and understand culture-dependent meanings with the aim of explaining employee behaviour. Rani intends to use the diagnostic focus groups with employees from different parts of the organisation who have already been mentored. Commensurate with her philosophical stance, she plans to bring together employees who work in similar positions, so that issues of power or fear of disclosing information are minimised. She is careful not to be overly structured in her approach, as she really wants to facilitate a flexible discussion. She anticipates the data will allow her to present a complex and rich picture of the new mentoring scheme.

Using semi-structured explanatory focus groups

The final design under semi-structured focus groups is that of an aid to examine quantitative or other results from a previous piece of research. This is not in terms of *validating* previous research, but to provide a means of interpreting or critically reappraising survey results. This can be done in the context of interpreting a survey carried out by another researcher or with your own survey results. Harrison (2013: 2157) describes explanatory designs as 'most often conducted when qualitative data are needed to help explain or build on initial quantitative data'. An example of using a focus group in this design is given in Box 2.6, where we also mention the use of online focus groups – this is examined in more detail in Chapter 3.

Box 2.6   Designing a semi-structured focus group as an explanatory aid

Sam is studying for an MBA and for his dissertation he is keen to survey higher education institutions to find out how they approach and manage joint ventures in international markets with other similar institutions. From his own experience of working in a university, he is aware that the market for such ventures is expanding and he is looking to understand the best way to establish and maintain a successful relationship. From his literature review, he has identified several topics which relate to his central research question, and has devised an online questionnaire to provide enough data to allow statistical analysis. He is happy with his questionnaire but on discussing the results with his supervisor he realises there are questions around managers' responses to the more personal aspect of the relationships in joint ventures. His quantitative data suggest this is a key aspect to the success of a joint venture so to explore this result further, Sam decides to run a synchronous (i.e. all participants contribute at the same time together) online focus group with a sample of the survey respondents to ask them specific questions about the importance of building relationships and how this actually occurs.

CRITERIA TO ASSESS THE QUALITY OF RESEARCH

For research involving focus groups, which is likely to be based on interpretive rather than positivist assumptions, we can use assessment criteria which are designed for qualitative research inquiry. These include dependability, credibility and transferability, which respectively parallel the more positivist criteria of reliability, validity and generalisability. For those who wish to use focus groups in a more positivist way, we first briefly outline these three assessment criteria.

Reliability

Reliability refers to replication and consistency of findings. Research is viewed as reliable if the measures used in data collection yield the same results as on other occasions, if similar observations are made, and there is transparency in how sense is created from the raw data (i.e. the focus group transcripts).

Validity

Validity can be explained as the degree to which a method really measures what it is supposed to measure. Internal validity refers to the extent to which findings can be attributed to intended interventions during the study, rather than to any flaws in research design. Focus groups are considered to be valid if they are used to research a problem that is suitable for focus group inquiry. Certainly, focus groups have a basic face validity, which means their findings look reasonable and believable. Discerning predictive validity, which indicates confirmation by future behaviour or events, is a little more difficult but has been demonstrated in studies which use mixed methods, for example comparing survey results and focus group findings, where the latter have demonstrated greater predictive validity.

Generalisability

Generalisability is also sometimes referred to as external validity, and means the extent to which findings are applicable to other settings. Krueger (1994) suggests that it is acceptable to make cautious generalisations if the focus group research has been carefully designed, conducted and analysed. So for example, concepts deriving from a study using focus groups might have relevance to other settings.

For researchers who are engaged in qualitative research based on interpretive assumptions, we now outline the three parallel criteria which can be used to assess the quality of such research.

Dependability

Dependability for a research inquiry relates to the process of how the research focus emerges and develops. A researcher would be looking to ensure transparency in their account of how the research progresses, making sure to keep a record which documents all the modifications made to the research focus over time. This serves to produce a dependable account which enables other people to understand and evaluate the emergent research.

Credibility

Credibility parallels the criterion of internal validity and indicates that there is equivalence between how the research participants' socially constructed realities have been represented by the researcher and what the participants themselves intended. Saunders et al. (2016) suggest a number of means to achieve such a match including: researching over a length of time to allow trust and rapport to develop, and to collect enough data; reflecting on the research process by discussing ideas or findings with another person; analysing data thoroughly, including any negative cases to present the optimum explanation of what is being studied; checking key elements of the research process (data, analysis, interpretations) with participants; and being careful to question one's own existing expectations about the research findings by continuously challenging these during data analysis, so that the participants' social constructions take priority.

Transferability

Transferability is the criterion which corresponds to generalisability or external validity, and involves the researcher making a clear and detailed description of the research as a whole. By providing such a full picture of all the elements of the research, including questions, design, context, findings and interpretation, the researcher allows others to judge whether the study may be transferable to a different setting.

For researchers who wish to delve more deeply into variances within broadly defined qualitative management research, there are more nuanced criteria for evaluation, contingent on particular philosophical assumptions (Johnson et al., 2006). In terms of choosing between the different types of criteria informed by positivist and interpretivist viewpoints, we suggest that you select the most appropriate set of criteria for your epistemological position.

SUMMARY OF FOCUS GROUP STRUCTURE AND PURPOSE

In this chapter we placed focus groups within the context of the researcher's philosophical assumptions. Such assumptions influence the choice of focus group and the kind of data it is intended to generate. For example, a researcher in search of objective data, who is informed by a positivist epistemology, may use a focus group as a precursor to a quantitative study. A researcher informed by a subjective approach to epistemology will seek to understand the realities of participants through focus groups and prioritise multiple meanings and interpretations. Hence, the focus group encounter in each of these contexts will not be the same and will generate different kinds of knowledge.

We also presented in this chapter the various ways in which focus groups might be structured to serve a particular research purpose, each illustrated with an example from the broad business and management field. We discussed how a research inquiry can be assessed using the appropriate criteria.

Thus, the researcher has several choices in how they design and use focus groups to answer a specific research question, building on their philosophical and epistemological considerations. Once that choice is made, the researcher can then turn their attention to the basic components of focus groups.

 **3**

BASIC COMPONENTS OF FOCUS GROUPS

INTRODUCTION

In Chapter 1 we defined focus groups as a technique used to explore a set of issues by allowing participants to discuss their experiences, opinions, feelings and ideas (Finch and Lewis, 2003), taking advantage of the interaction found in a group setting. Conducting successful focus groups requires careful consideration of a number of points linked to the planning process as this is where focus groups depart most from other qualitative methods (Morgan, 1997). This chapter will give the reader an overview of the tools and techniques required prior to running an actual focus group. As such we cover format decisions, the discussion agenda and practicalities including sampling and composition, recruitment, size and number of groups, timeframe, budget and location, before introducing the pilot stage.

FOCUS GROUP FORMAT DECISIONS

Advancement in today's technological environment has affected the way we perceive and conduct research, and focus groups are no exception (Tuttas, 2015). The method is no longer practised merely in its archetypal form of face-to-face contact, but its online variations have also captured the attention of researchers. Mobile applications, telephone and teleconferencing focus groups, webcam focus groups, online journaling, and communities and social media all mean that focus groups can be utilised in new ways (McDermott, 2013). We now briefly discuss the most prevalent focus group formats.

Face-to-face focus groups

Face-to-face focus groups involve inviting approximately four to twelve participants to discuss a particular topic, in an arranged physical setting with the active presence of a moderator. Traditionally, focus groups have been implemented in such a face-to-face situation where participants and the moderator engage in a discussion for one to two hours in an enclosed space (Nicholas et al., 2010). The main advantage of this traditional focus group format is the capture of non-verbal communication and reactions of participants which essentially enhance the quality and depth of the data (Brüggen and Willems, 2009). The visual cues in focus groups comprise an important element in data collection, analysis and reporting as they encapsulate the group element and feel. Furthermore, moderators in face-to-face focus groups can observe the 'life cycle' of the discussion, as it becomes evident from body language when participants are tired or excited about a topic and moderators can react accordingly. As some groups surpass two hours it is not unusual to witness signs of fatigue, such as participants lying back on their chair, or looking constantly at the time and shortening their answers, and thus indicating their desire to wrap up the discussion and go home. In a face-to-face setting the moderator has the advantage of observation, not only of each group member but also of the group as a whole, and can react accordingly. Of course, there are disadvantages in face-to-face groups compared to other formats. Face-to-face focus groups are often seen as time consuming, costly and requiring much effort to organise and run. Additionally, face-to-face focus groups encounter recruitment barriers, especially when the sample is geographically dispersed such as participants who live in rural areas, have uncommon health problems, find it difficult to access the venue due to mobility issues or perceive the entire face-to-face discussion setting as uncomfortable and intimidating (Nicholas et al., 2010). Despite these disadvantages, Stewart and Shamdasani (2015) acknowledge that face-to-face focus group discussions remain the most commonly used form of in-depth research. However, there are other ways focus groups can be run.

Telephone focus groups and variations

The disadvantages of face-to-face focus groups have shifted a number of researchers towards other formats of the method, such as telephone focus groups. Like face-to-face focus groups, telephone focus groups are a type of qualitative data collection technique that uses the group process as a central source of data with a moderator who actively guides the discussion (Allen, 2014).

Technically, telephone focus groups may not need any special equipment and they resemble a conference call. There is the option of a more sophisticated approach using consoles with lights and name tags to identify participants, special switching devices that allow only one participant to talk at a time and lights indicating that participants want to express their opinion (Krueger, 1994). However, advanced tel-econferencing facilities may not be accessible to all participants. For this reason, researchers may complement this method with online options such as webinars, with or without the use of a web camera. For instance, Chong et al. (2015) added a webinar platform via Adobe® Connect™ to their telephone focus group study. Participants logged into the webinar using the links they were given and saw differ-ent display panels on their screens, such as participants' and webinar hosts' names and a main display pod which was used to display information from the moderator. The webinar facility allowed participants to choose a status (I agree, I disagree), 'raise a hand' for questions or comments, and feed back to the rest of the partici-pants through the telephone, which facilitated group interaction. The authors found the experience rewarding in terms of quality of data and stated that this option is a good alternative to face-to-face groups.

Telephone focus groups differ from face-to-face focus groups in that they tend to be smaller, with four to six participants. The moderator also needs to be more active in encouraging discussion and triggering interaction and very much alert to para-verbal cues, such as emphasis, laughter and voice variations (Hurworth, 2005). One of the advantages of telephone focus groups is gaining access to participants in dis-persed geographical locations. For example, Allen (2014) conducted telephone focus groups with mental health consultants who worked with rural and urban Head Start programmes in Alaska and Oregon in order to explore their perspectives on develop-ing positive partnerships with early care and education staff. Additionally, this type of focus group can eliminate the need for meeting facilities, catering and travelling costs, and thus reduce the overall cost of running focus groups. It is also easier to accommo-date tight work schedules and so makes it more likely that some participants like busy managers will take part in the research. This type of format seems easier to handle given that participants are more likely to take turns when they talk. The increased level of anonymity makes this method attractive with sensitive topics by creating a psychological distance and thus 'safe' environment for participants. Finally, it is pos-sible to run more groups in a day whereas with face-to-face focus groups this would be unrealistic. At the same time this format has also been criticised due to the lack of visual cues which reduce social presence and compromise spontaneous discussion which may lead to limited interaction during the discussions (Gothberg et al., 2013). Sampling bias may also be seen as a problem as participants are limited to those hav-ing the equipment (Smith et al., 2009). There is a necessity for more 'control' over the discussion and most commentators suggest a co-facilitator who can assist with the social interaction, for example the speaker identification process (Hurworth, 2005). In summary, the method overcomes a few challenges of the traditional format and is seen as as effective as face-to-face focus groups for factual information exchange and information gathering.

Online focus groups

Technological advances have enabled researchers to explore the potential of focus groups in an online environment (Woodyatt et al., 2016). Online focus groups may be distinguished from other focus group formats as they utilise information and digital technology (Abrams et al., 2015). There are two main types of online focus groups in terms of how these are conducted: asynchronous and synchronous focus groups.

Asynchronous online focus groups

This type of focus group format involves bulletin boards, email-type correspondence (Deggs et al., 2010) and typically 12 to 20 respondents. It is conducted over a period of time and does not require a simultaneous online presence (Sweet, 2001). The moderator starts a discussion thread and keeps participants involved with probing questions and provides a timeframe for responses. Because such groups do not require participants to be simultaneously online, they can be easier to arrange (Liamputtong, 2011). Asynchronous online focus groups are typically conducted on web boards or other web forums, access to which can be limited to those invited by the researcher (Deggs et al., 2010) and do not need transcribing as the moderator can download and save the scripts. Google groups and Ning are good examples for hosting such groups and are easily accessible by researchers. This format has its advantages in terms of outreach, no need for transcription, and facilitated identification of each participant. One of the main disadvantages is the longer timeframe needed to complete the focus group discussions, a key consideration for graduate dissertation projects. Other disadvantages include their unsuitability for group activities which require participants to work together; the lack of visual cues, which affects group interaction; uncertainty about the origin of the provided information as the moderator cannot verify whether the same participant is generating the information; and sampling bias as participation is limited to those who have access to online platforms.

Synchronous online focus groups

Synchronous online focus groups indicate that all respondents are online at the same time and respond to the moderator's questions (Woodyatt et al., 2016). In other words, the moderator and the participants are in an online chat room simultaneously and type their comments which are visible to the group. The moderator can download the script at the end of the discussion. This type of online focus group usually consists of four to nine participants who are assigned a username to join a chat room and a moderator to guide the discussion. Participants can withdraw from the conversation at any point.

There are two variations of online synchronous focus groups. One option is to invite participants to a chat room by selecting an online platform or a mobile app (e.g. WeChat, WhatsApp). This option will have similar advantages to asynchronous focus groups, such as anonymity as the participants will not be visible to the group. There are a few disadvantages: inability to develop a holistic view of who is writing and thus a profile of the participant; difficulties in understanding participants in terms of interaction during the discussion; and challenges in terms of visual cues and understanding the extent to which people are enthusiastic or critical about a topic or concept (Scholl et al., 2002). The recent popularity of chat emoticons can address concerns relating to the emotions of participants when discussing particular issues as they have an option to use happy faces ☺, sad ones ☹ and a range in between.

The second option with online synchronous focus groups is to use this format with a webcam or a webcam alone with no chatting facilities. The participants do not need special software, other than an online platform such as Skype or Adobe® Connect™ and only meet online at the provided link. This can be done with no financial cost (e.g. via Skype) or other more sophisticated paid applications/software. Overall, there are a few advantages associated with online synchronous focus groups that include budget savings, time and access to international settings and having notes to hand straight after the session (Scholl et al., 2002). Nevertheless, the method has received criticism related to recruitment, lack of interaction and visual cues, and sampling as it requires more careful screening than in face-to-face groups, for example to confirm a participant's age group.

Online and face-to-face focus groups share similarities, for example the moderator initiates the discussion, asks questions and clarifications, and follows the discussion agenda (Brüggen and Willems, 2009). Woodyatt et al. (2016) compared synchronous online focus groups and face-to-face focus groups and their findings illustrate that although the format of the generated data may differ (for example, word count) the content of the data generated is remarkably similar.

In Box 3.1 we present an example of using online synchronous focus groups which illustrates the challenges of this particular format.

Box 3.1   Arranging an online synchronous focus group

Daniel is studying for a masters in Marketing Management and Practice and wants to use his dissertation to explore online factors influencing word of mouth on fast moving consumer goods. Daniel acknowledges the limited information available on the topic and wants to use focus groups to gain insight on the topic and then inform the design of an online questionnaire. He decides to use online synchronous focus groups with Skype as he believes that the recruiting process will be greatly facilitated by allowing participants to discuss the topic in their own preferred location.

He also believes that his background in education will prove useful when moderating the discussions. Daniel has prepared the discussion guide and has recruited participants via social media. His recruiting experience has been very positive as within a few days six participants agreed to be part of his focus group discussions. He carefully considers time differences (two participants are in a different country) and suggests a time and day that would fit in with his own and the participants' schedule. He decides to run the first group and emails all the participants with details of the discussion including his Skype username. However, from six participants only two show up and Daniel faces one of the biggest fears of moderators: the case of the 'no show'. Daniel is very disappointed but also learns a great deal from this experience. He learns that participants may need more than one reminder; over-recruiting – especially in online formats – is a good idea if not a necessity; and organising a focus group is not as easy as he anticipated.

Focus groups in virtual worlds

A further variation of the online format which has gained popularity and represents great opportunities for the method in the future is the use of avatars in virtual worlds (Gadalla et al., 2016). A virtual world is a computer-generated, multi-user, 3D interface in which each user interacts with the environment through his or her individual avatar, which is a graphic representation personified by means of computer technology (Holzwarth et al., 2006). In other words, the moderator and the participants have their own avatars and meet in a virtual chat room and start the discussion, which is recorded with text capturing. According to Gadalla et al. (2016) one such virtual platform is Second Life, currently used by brands like Coca Cola and IBM, that offers a glimpse of the 3D internet of the future by allowing virtual conferencing and meetings in spaces provided by the platform. The authors suggest that there is no evident difference in data quality between the results of avatar focus groups and face-to-face focus groups.

Making a format decision

As we have illustrated, researchers have a wide range of choice in terms of focus group format and it would be advisable to consider the following points to help make a decision. The objectives of the research, how much time is available for the project, the location and accessibility of participants, and the type of participant required should all be considered. Additional factors like availability of budget, as well as the sensitivity of the topic, will also influence format choice. In summary, the researcher needs to evaluate carefully which format best fits the project.

DESIGNING THE FOCUS GROUP DISCUSSION AGENDA

In this section we discuss the importance of a well-designed and piloted focus group discussion agenda. The discussion agenda or discussion guide, also sometimes referred to as a protocol, is an outline of topics or questions that the moderator intends to cover. Krueger (1998) encourages beginner moderators to avoid a topic guide option and to take a questioning route. In other words, experienced moderators may note the overall topics and expand them during the group discussions whereas other less experienced moderators may find it more helpful to formulate specific questions and cover them during the discussions. In the case of research projects, the discussion agenda is usually the result of an extensive literature review, identification of research gaps and formulation of topics or questions. Most importantly researchers need to be clear about the inquiry and be able to transfer it into main research questions. One of the challenges in research projects is being able to articulate and coherently form the themes into questions. Good preparation and piloting of not only the discussion agenda but also the overall focus group process are important.

We distinguish three main areas to consider for the discussion agenda: technical, such as number and type of questions, and forming and phrasing questions; delivery, including sequencing and probing questions; and enrichment activities and techniques.

Technical issues

Selecting and formulating questions are issues that the researcher needs to consider for good discussions. Merton et al. (1956) highlight the importance of discussing a range of topics that not only cover the known issues but also bring up ones that have not been anticipated (see also Chapter 1 where we discuss range). One way of doing this is by brainstorming, which was proposed by Osborn (1957) as an effective technique for improving productivity and creativity during group decision making. Researchers can brainstorm (with their groups or supervisors or even friends) and collect a range of topics linked to their research project and select the ones that they need to form into questions. Morgan (1997) cautions that too often researchers limit the discussion by making their own assumptions about important issues. In an early focus group project one of the authors looked at consumer perceptions of green claims in advertising. In identifying the range of topics to address, one important area was not considered for the discussion agenda: recycling routines. Yet, most participants made clear connections between the two topics and initiated recycling routine discussions. As the moderator had not included the topic in the agenda she actively shifted the discussion away from recycling only to realise while analysing and reporting the findings that one of the parameters in being aware of green claims is recycling practice.

A draft including a range of topics or questions will emerge after the brainstorming session(s). One of the most frequently asked questions by researchers is 'How many questions are enough?'. This is difficult to answer as it largely depends on various factors such as the structure of the groups, the timeframe and the schedules, and the planned activities during the group discussions. Krueger (1998) argues that the rule of thumb depends on the nature of the questions as some questions take less discussion time than others. He recommends consideration of the questions in terms of minutes with some questions taking five and others 10 or 15 minutes, all depending on the stage of the discussion and their importance to the study. Overall, researchers should plan for a 90-minute to two-hour session and keep some extra questions as a backup in case the group is not as talkative as expected and there is some time left to cover a few extra questions.

We suggest that moderators invest time during the initial stage of the focus group to ask participants some introductory questions. The aim of these initial questions is twofold: to break the ice and make rapport with the participants, and gather some basic information about the participants (voice, name) in order to facilitate transcription later on. Such questions do not offer great information for data analysis but can encourage participation and sharing. For instance, in our focus groups on consumer shopping priorities we asked participants to share with us a few things about themselves, where they lived and whether they enjoyed shopping. This way we matched participants to a voice, useful when transcribing, and they opened up about their shopping preferences. The moderator can use this part of the discussion to introduce the research to participants, explaining purpose, who is funding the study, confidentiality and process. Usually, moderators at this point set the 'rules' and remind participants that every opinion counts and encourage them to switch off their mobile phones and enjoy the discussion (see Chapter 4 where we discuss conducting the focus group).

Krueger (1998) suggests a few transition questions come next, where the moderator shifts the conversation towards the main topic of discussion. So for our study on consumer shopping priorities, we asked participants to share a recent shopping story at their preferred retailer, thus bringing them closer to the main focus of the discussion. Following these transition questions are the key focus questions where the aim is to cover the important themes that need to be addressed. In our experience these types of questions require the majority of time and we usually include some activities for the participants. A few of our key questions for the research topic on shopping included: Can you take us through the decision process when you bought brand Y? Why did you buy product Y? What are the most important features of brand Y? The summary and ending questions offer the moderator the opportunity to acquire a summary and/or closing statement from the participants. In our discussions we find it useful to ask every participant to share a final thought, recommendation, message or suggestion for the focus of the study. So in our shopping study we asked them to summarise the main points or give some advice/a message to brand managers. Finally, we find it useful to ask if anyone wants to add something before we formally end the discussion.

The challenge with the discussion agenda is not only deciding how many and what type of questions but formulating comprehensible questions. Well-formulated and structured questions do not require an explanation or further clarification and no moderator wants to hear for an answer: What do you mean? Investing time in formulating questions that are well structured in both grammar and syntax can take the discussion a long way.

Most focus group moderators prefer open-ended questions as they are able to generate discussion. Thus, it is more productive to ask 'How did you feel about your shopping experience?' than 'Are you satisfied with your shopping experience?'. Krueger (1998) acknowledges that closed questions may be used in the later parts of the discussion but we also find them useful at the start of the discussion if, for example, we want to identify shopping decision makers in our groups. Questions also need to be kept simple and straightforward and adjusted to the group of participants. It is advisable to avoid complex vocabulary where possible. We find that participants are confused when asked about their 'eco labelling perceptions' and respond much better when asked how they feel about the Fair Trade label, for instance, on their favourite brand of coffee.

Delivery

Other than technical issues there are a number of elements relating to the delivery of the discussion agenda. As such, the sequence of the questions is important and, according to Krueger (1998), is a hallmark of focus group interviews and 'sets the word "focus" in the title' (p. 37). A well-planned sequence of questions allows the discussion to flow naturally and the moderator to cover in-depth important research themes before moving along. For instance, when discussing shopping priorities, we start from more general themes and move to more specific ones: Can you take us through one of your weekend shopping expeditions? What makes you buy product Y? What are your favourite features of product R? Participants have the opportunity to share their stories and listen to the rest of the group and make reflections and comparisons. This is also a way of moving from more general questions to more specific ones as the moderator needs to establish the context before focusing on specific questions (Krueger, 1998). Having follow-up questions means that participants will have the chance to answer in more depth. It is also important to remember that participants will at some time offer vague answers or incomplete stories and the role of the moderator is to probe them in order to elicit additional information (Krueger, 1998) and make the required clarifications. Finally, moderators need to be able to distinguish the actual experiences from the discussed generalities. Asking participants about their own experiences and stories and prompting for details and facts will provide focus for the discussion as well as interesting data for analysis.

Enrichment activities and techniques

Finally, moderators have an option of using tools and activities which may circumvent potential barriers to expression (Krueger, 1998). These are one of the great advantages of face-to-face focus groups as they have the potential to utilise various activities which have been termed as 'engaging questions' (Krueger, 1998), 'focusing exercises' (Bloor et al., 2001) or 'activity-oriented questions' (Colucci, 2007). These terms connote a similar concept: an activity-based interaction amongst the participants. These include, but are not limited to: making lists, rating, choosing among alternatives, arranging categories, conceptual mapping and sorting photos. The use of visuals in research has been considered an effective way of exploring people's constructs as words conjure up associated images and vice versa (Stiles, 2004). Participants have the chance to draw their own representations or comment on existing ones. It is important that editing is avoided during analysis and that the pictorial constructs are accompanied by the related discussion (Stiles, 2004). Brondani et al. (2008) combined focus groups and vignettes to discuss oral health and disability and were pleased with the combination of the two. They reported rich discussions, with plenty of interaction and participation.

In Box 3.2 we present two examples of using activities drawing on our own consumer research.

Box 3.2   Activities in focus groups: conceptual mapping and drawing

In our research on consumers' perceptions of eco-friendly products we wanted to explore how British consumers define a green product. We incorporated Krueger's (1998) conceptual mapping into the group discussions. This allows participants to describe a green product in relation to similar product characteristics using their own classification system. For this activity we displayed a number of different products on the table and gave participants five minutes to classify the products on an A4 sheet of paper. Participants produced similar classifications which they shared with the group. After everyone presented their categories the moderator asked about differences and commonalities in classifications. This activity produced a great deal of information about the factors that participants prioritise in terms of green product purchasing which may vary from price, to quality and aesthetics. As Krueger (1998) notes, the greater insights come from the discussion and justification of the categories. This activity was suitable for our purpose as our research dealt with a specific and tangible topic such as daily shopping where participants can launch straight into the exercise whereas in more abstract topics the moderator would offer some 'help'

(Continued)

(Continued)

such as lists on a flipchart (Krueger, 1998). In another project we explored French consumers' perceptions of eco labels in Paris and used a similar activity. One of our research questions was 'How do consumers visualise the ideal eco label in terms of shape, size and colour?'. We decided to investigate this research question by providing A4 drawing pads and crayons to our participants. The results surprised us, as participants visualised and drew eco labels similar to the ones in the market that they had previously strongly rejected as misleading. This offered a fruitful discussion in terms of visual meanings and informed our semiotic analysis of eco labelling and product packaging in Paris.

Projective techniques

Projective techniques can be used for generating qualitative data, especially with sensitive topics when participants may be reluctant to share their views (Pich and Dean, 2015). They are relatively easy to administer and able to capture valuable responses (Nurkka et al., 2009). Such techniques include but are not limited to: word associations, where participants associate words with other words, concepts or meanings; sentence/drawing completion, where participants are asked to complete a task (see the example of using visual techniques in Box 2.2); and drawing, where participants draw and discuss. Researchers using techniques and activities need to ensure that the understanding generated reflects the imagery and associations of the participants (Pich and Dean, 2015), as projective techniques can be seen as ambiguous (Pettigrew and Charters, 2008) and time consuming, generating limited responses (Langford and McDonagh, 2003).

In some cases, marketing researchers or practitioners need to work with external stimuli and material in order to elicit project-specific responses. These vary from product packages, samples, posters and advertisements to concepts and written statements. In some of our focus groups we use external stimuli, usually products. At some point in the discussion, we display a number of products on the table for participants to look at, touch and comment upon. The timing of the product display needs to be carefully considered as it is one of the moments that may generate a 'mini chaos' in the groups and some reactions and comments may be lost. Video recording can help here. Participants typically make important comments when they first hold or see the materials and the moderator needs to be alert. We usually give our participants a few minutes to look at the displayed products. From our experience, transcribing this part of the discussion is a challenge, and moderators are advised to repeat the product's name each time a participant expresses a view to facilitate transcription.

In Box 3.3 we outline an example of a discussion agenda highlighting the types of questions raised above.

Box 3.3   Example of a discussion agenda

Introductory questions by the moderator –
ice breakers and introduction

My name is Julie and I am a researcher exploring consumer perceptions of product labels in various European countries. We will spend the next couple of hours discussing your experience and perceptions of labels found on your favourite products. We will also do some activities. Please keep in mind that no specific knowledge is required, so feel free to share your opinions, which are highly valued, but most importantly enjoy the discussion. At this point we can all switch off/put on silent mode our phones, switch on the audio recorder and start by taking turns introducing yourselves [...]

Introduction to main discussion questions

Can you briefly talk about your weekly food shopping routine? [...]

Can you recall and share your most recent food shopping experience?

What kind of information were you looking for whilst shopping for the X product you just mentioned?

[Follow up: Which type of information do you value the most? Why?]

Can you list the top five priorities when you shop for this type of product?

Transition questions

When you purchased product X did you happen to notice any piece of environmental information?

Alexandre, you mentioned environmental information as one of your priorities. Can you elaborate?

Can anyone recall other types of environmental information on products?

[....]

Argyro, you make an interesting point there, can the rest of the group share their own experience?

Key focus question

How do you understand this label: Fair Trade?

(Continued)

(Continued)

Activity: word association

Please provide equivalent word(s) for the following: recyclable, CFCs, ozone friendly, ozone safe.

Justify and expand on your associations.

Activity: sketching/drawing

Please draw your ideal environmental logo. Use colours and shapes. You can use one of these product packages and stick it on the product.

Justify your choice.

Closure: summary and ending questions

What is your message to the manufacturer of this product in terms of the product logo? Would anyone like to add something before we end the discussion?

[closing remarks and farewells]

DESIGNING FOCUS GROUPS: SOME PRACTICALITIES

Planning focus groups involves a number of decisions the researcher must address carefully before conducting the discussions. Bringing together a number of participants and deciding on the mode of interaction can be challenging and determines the type of data collected. Thus, in this section we outline some practical decisions researchers need to address before the start of the sessions, to help ensure that focus groups run smoothly and generate rich data. As such we discuss sampling and composition, recruitment options, size and number of groups, timeframe, location and budget considerations.

Sampling and composition

Researchers need to consider their sampling strategy as it determines the quality of data gathered as well as the comparisons that can be made. Flick (2014) suggests that the general issue underpinning sampling decisions is how to select cases from the wider population so that the findings apply not just to the participants but to the research area. In other words, the aim of the focus groups is to draw some inferences about a population of interest and thus the groups must consist of representative members of that population (Stewart and Shamdasani, 2015). At this point we need to stress that 'representative members' does not indicate statistical representativeness of a population but it is about representing members of a population which may be of interest to the study. It is more the case with qualitative research that the individuals, their characteristics and background are relevant for sampling decisions and the researcher may need (or need to mix) specific types of individuals. Some common demographic segmentation variables are gender, ethnicity, age and social class. Patton (2015) argues that the different logic underpinning sampling approaches is where qualitative and quantitative methods differ the most, as quantitative methods typically depend on larger samples selected randomly as opposed to qualitative inquiry which focuses in-depth on relatively small samples selected purposively.

Purposive sampling is commonly used in focus group research (Morgan, 1997) and allows the data to be interrogated purposively in terms of making comparisons (Barbour, 2007) or encouraging the researchers to go beyond the familiar voices and findings (MacNaghten and Myers, 2004). Barbour (2007) mentions that qualitative sampling is either theoretical or purposive and essentially the process is the same: theorising at an early stage about the dimensions that are likely to be relevant in terms of giving rise to different perceptions and experiences. As such researchers need to think about the relevant criteria early in their study and make the most appropriate sampling decision. Researchers may also need to reflect on the kind of participants needed for the study (e.g. managers, families) and their schedule requirements before inviting them to take part in the research.

Stewart and Shamdasani (2015) suggest that convenience sampling can be employed, which has many advantages. The researcher can save considerable time and resources without compromising group characteristics and at the same time achieve the desired group interaction. Researchers usually look at their existing networks when considering participant selection for their focus groups and their pilot study. Snowball or chain sampling is where researchers seek participants by asking well-situated people or known networks 'Who should I talk to?' (Patton, 2015). In our research with SMEs and environmental management systems we ran focus groups with SME managers in the north of the UK using snowball sampling, asking our focus group members to suggest potential future participants. This is useful when researching smaller organisations where recruiting managers can be a challenge.

One important group composition decision is whether there is a need for homogeneous or heterogeneous groups in terms of the background (Morgan, 1997). There are advantages and disadvantages to running homogeneous groups as participants share common characteristics and the discussion is comparable.

For instance, if cultural differences are the focus of the research then recruiting participants according to ethnicity allows for better comparisons. Another important decision is related to strangers or acquaintances. Both present their own advantages and dynamics, taking the researcher back to the project objectives. Morgan and Krueger (1993) break the myth of participants having to be strangers and mention that in social sciences focus groups are routinely conducted within contexts in which acquaintanceship is unavoidable, for instance in an organisational setting.

In one of our projects on misleading chlorofluorocarbon logos on product packaging we recruited two senior managers and three employees from different departments in an organisation and witnessed the power relationships in medium-sized organisations. We had participants from marketing (marketing manager), the technical department (TQM manager) and R&D (three employees). This was a fruitful experience as we witnessed a debate amongst the various departments in an organisation. The technical department manager argued that the marketing department displayed misleading claims by blindly following existing market trends. The marketing manager stressed the usefulness of promoting environmental sustainability on product packaging as a response to existing consumer trends. The R&D employees discussed how senior managers gave them little space to comment on labelling matters.

In summary, when considering sampling and composition, it is important that potential participants have the common experience that is the key to the research focus.

Recruitment

Recruiting participants has become less time consuming and easier with the access potential of online platforms, communities and social media. Researchers need to be aware that at the same time this facilitation can turn into a limitation if screening is not done carefully, especially with online formats of the method. Researchers can recruit participants starting from their informal networks by going through various social media platforms, online communities and so on. In our research with SME managers we initially used existing lists from the chamber of commerce and membership institutions and emailed potential participants. MacDougall and Fudge (2001) propose a three-step approach in terms of recruitment: 'prepare', where the researcher drafts the ways to construct a sample and becomes familiar with similar projects and design elements; 'contact' where the researcher starts contacting key participants who may be able to suggest other participants; and 'follow-up' where the researcher needs to maintain involvement. In Box 3.4 we outline an example of a recruitment questionnaire we developed for our research on environmental labelling on fast moving consumer goods in the UK.

Box 3.4 Example of a recruitment questionnaire

Good morning/afternoon/evening. We are carrying out some research about product labelling. Would you mind answering a few questions for us?

Q 1. Please look at these statements and tell me which one applies to you.

1. I always do the household shopping at the supermarket.
2. I share the household shopping with my partner but go to the supermarket on a regular basis.
3. We go to the supermarket together most of the time to do the household shopping.
4. I tend to leave my partner to do the household shopping and rarely go to the supermarket.

(Close if respondent agrees with statement 4.)

Q 2. Which of these supermarkets do you use for a) main shopping; b) top-up shopping? (recruit a spread)

ASDA Aldi Co-op Kwiksave Lidl

Morrisons Tesco Safeway Sainsbury's

Q 3. How many times per week do you visit this type of retailer?

Q4. Basic demographic questions:

Name

Age group (please circle as appropriate) 20-34 35-49 50-64 65+

Contact details (telephone number and email)

Occupation

Marital status (please indicate number of children if applicable)

Notes to recruiters:

All respondents must be involved in the main household shopping (ie. must regularly do the supermarket shopping either on their own or with their partner).

All respondents must have been born and brought up in the UK. Recruit 8 per group. Groups will last 2 hours. Incentive £30

Signature

Date

Finally, as we illustrated in Box 3.1 it is useful to over-recruit as it is common for a few participants not to show up.

Size of groups

Focus group texts typically suggest up to 12 participants although we think fewer than 12 is easier to manage. Krueger (1994) reports the greatest success with six to eight participants, perhaps even fewer for complex issues. Kinnear and Taylor (1996) state that having more than eight people within a focus group tends to diminish the opportunity for some respondents to participate. Morgan (1997) suggests that when the topic is emotionally charged fewer members can be recruited which can generate high levels of participant involvement, while larger groups seem more appropriate with neutral topics that generate lower levels of involvement. In our research on consumers' perceptions of organic products we recruited ten participants per group which presented a challenge in terms of managing group dynamics and the flow of the discussion. Towards the end of the discussions in one group, participants were speaking simultaneously, creating pairs and mini groups and even arranging a future get-together. This type of activity becomes a problem for the moderator who needs to keep the discussion focused and clear as the conversation becomes impossible to transcribe and may result in missing content. For academic research the analysis depends on attributing specific sets of interaction to group members which becomes more challenging in large group settings. Finally, hard-to-access participants such as senior executives require some effort and time to recruit, and arranging large focus groups may be unrealistic. Conflicts of time schedules and responsibilities make it hard for individuals to participate.

Number of groups

A key question which is often raised by researchers when debating the use of focus groups is 'How many focus groups should I do?'. There is no single response to this question, as it depends on several factors such as the purpose of the research, and the constraints of finances and time. Many authors agree that between three and six is an appropriate number but this depends on the complexity of the topic (Morgan with Scannell, 1998). Some research topics have incorporated over 30 focus groups but for a masters dissertation such a research design would be unfeasible. In practice, it is difficult to predict how many groups this will take. In a study by Brici et al. (2013), it was found that saturation, which they define as the moderator being able to anticipate what the participants are going to say, was reached after three focus groups each with adolescents and adults. In a study on firm–employee relationships by Herington et al. (2005), they found that after the third focus group, participants were repeating information that had already been gathered from previous groups. They held a further focus group as a final confirmation, but the process ceased at this point as no new information was provided by the members of this group. Another important consideration when deciding the number of groups is the research objective and the role of the focus group in the overall project methodology. The number of groups may depend on whether focus groups are used as a stand-alone method or as a method together with a survey which would require fewer groups. With a very small number of groups it will be difficult to claim patterning of the data (Barbour, 2007) as comparability is limited. Also the more segmented the groups (age, gender, ethnicity) the more groups will be needed to reach saturation. A common solution is to proceed until no new data emerges; in other words the last group simply repeats previous contributions and so saturation is reached (Lunt and Livingstone, 1996).

Timeframe and budget

Tight dissertation and assignment deadlines require consistent and careful timeframe planning as focus groups can be time consuming at almost every stage. One of the most time intensive activities is recruiting and successfully bringing together a number of participants on a specific day and time for the discussions. Recruiting participants can be extremely time consuming even if online platforms have made access to some categories of participants easier. The focus group discussions themselves can take longer than a typical individual interview and a two-hour slot may be a safe assumption. It is advisable to leave a gap not less than a day between the focus groups as debriefing, transcribing and reflecting straight after each discussion can be beneficial in terms of analysis. Researchers are advised to put aside a generous amount of time to code and analyse transcripts, the moderator's notes and any data generated by the various focus group activities. Finally, the timeframe in terms of recruitment, transcription and running focus groups reduces with online formats as discussed in previous sections.

Focus groups can be an expensive method, and careful planning of resources is deemed essential. It is unlikely that graduate researchers will need to hire special venue facilities, use a professional moderator or offer cash incentives as practised in market research agencies. A few budget considerations are transportation to and from the venue, refreshments for participants and a good quality recording device. Prompts may be needed for any activities. A checklist with important items is useful. We provide such a checklist in Box 3.5.

Box 3.5   Example of a moderator checklist

A recorder with extra batteries or a portable charger

Discussion agenda

Incentives (if applicable)

(Continued)

(Continued)

Consent forms and a few spare information sheets

Spare pens

Name tags or labels

A3 sheets

Any required stimuli such as products

Camera to photograph activities, such as product groupings

Mobile phone in case participants call to cancel or notify for late arrival

Location

Most researchers believe the physical setting and venue are very important to the effectiveness of the group session (Carey, 1994). In online variations of the method the venue is usually an online platform such as Skype or a chat room. Selecting a good venue for face-to-face focus groups will create the desired atmosphere for comfortable discussions. Important elements are the ventilation, lighting, acoustics, seating arrangements, space and equipment if necessary. The atmosphere should include a relaxed feeling, so that informal and spontaneous comments are encouraged (Kinnear and Taylor, 1996). Graduate researchers typically conduct focus groups on campus or in quiet cafes or restaurants as their own and their participants' safety need to remain a priority. Overall, the venue needs to be accessible to the focus group participants to reduce the chances of people not turning up. If the venue is unknown to the participants, providing detailed directions is highly advisable. Finally, as Bloor et al. (2001) point out, there is no such thing as a neutral venue for focus group research as participants may demonstrate different kinds of behaviour in different venues (e.g. in a familiar coffee shop as opposed to a hotel conference room). The most important element other than the seating arrangements and the comfort of the participants is the ability to record effectively and as clearly as possible.

PILOTING THE FOCUS GROUP

Once the planning stage has been completed, a pilot study is advised as you might encounter unforeseen problems and may need to adjust your introduction or choose a different venue. You may need to rethink the ideal size of the group or the duration of the discussions. Most importantly it is a chance to test the discussion agenda and make any required adjustments. Following completion of the pilot focus group you are ready to start the main study.

SUMMARY

In this chapter we have discussed some basic focus group design considerations including focus group format, designing the agenda, and many other practicalities such as size and number of groups. At this point we echo Morgan (1997) and other focus group commentators and stress that the aim of this chapter (and the following one) is not to create an 'abc guide to conducting focus groups' as there is no one right way of designing and conducting focus groups. Rather, researchers need to make their own informed decisions according to the type of project, their research objectives and the available timeframe. In Chapter 4 we look at the focus group process itself, and how the components can be operationalised in the collection of data.

 **4**

CONDUCTING FOCUS GROUPS

INTRODUCTION

In the previous chapter we focused on the components related to focus group design. In this chapter we consider the conduct of the focus group itself. Thus, we discuss key issues linked to the focus group process, such as the important role of the moderator and the level of moderator involvement in the discussions; ethical procedures and considerations; the various focus group strategies and dynamics; practicalities during and after the focus groups such as transcription and translation; and challenging moments when things just go wrong!

THE FOCUS GROUP MODERATOR

Focus group experts agree that the role of the moderator is not predictable nor fixed (Greenbaum, 2000), as his or her tasks are not standardised but vary depending on factors such as the moderator's experience and skills, and the nature of the project. For example, as we saw in Chapter 2, focus groups can be underpinned by different philosophical assumptions, which will affect how the researcher approaches the moderation. The researcher intending to run a focus group from a positivist stance is likely to remain objective and distanced from the process, in an effort to minimise influencing the participants. A moderator informed by a more interpretivist stance may well see the focus group as an interactive event, where both moderator and participants co-construct the process. Here, considerations of the moderator's role and influence will form part of the research inquiry and be reflected upon in the dissertation.

There are advantages to moderating your own focus groups rather than asking someone else to take the role. We find that moderating brings the researcher closer to the data and assists greatly with the transcription and analysis phases. The moderator becomes a first-hand witness to the general 'feel' of the group, the expressed body language, the discussion and the occasional jokes or arguments, and generally is empowered to cover the discussion agenda and subsequently address the research questions. It is common for moderators to recall the source of a specific comment or joke, the group dynamics and the level of participants' engagement with the topics. The moderator can recall particular quotes that are important for project presentation purposes. We find ourselves listening to our past focus group recordings and being able to recall details of the groups such as names of participants, particular comments and other important elements of the discussions. Finally, moderating the groups assists the translation and/or transcription processes which are time-consuming elements of the focus group method.

Moderator skills and characteristics

Focus group literature has identified a number of professional qualities and individual characteristics or skills of moderators that may influence the outcome of the focus group discussions (Greenbaum, 2000). Moderators need relevant expertise, experience, educational background, group dynamic management skills and interviewing techniques that are essential in order to 'peel away the onion' (Greenbaum, 2000: 27) and access attitudes, perceptions and behaviours (Stewart and Shamdasani, 2015). Professional moderators are experienced in both dimensions of focus group moderation: handling the dynamics of the group whilst exploring in depth the research questions (Greenbaum, 2000). In other words, moderators manage both the participants and the research agenda while remaining impartial (if desired) and supportive.

Sharing information between moderator and participants

At this point we need to stress the importance of a moderator being careful with providing examples, making humorous comments and expressing emotion. Both Krueger (1998) and Greenbaum (2000) state that this may constrict the range of participants' responses as they will want to agree with the moderator. However, in some situations, sharing factual or demographic information about themselves may seem acceptable, for example to empathise with participants. In Box 4.1 we give an example from an MBA dissertation we supervised where the MBA student, acting as moderator for their own focus groups, overshared information with the participants both verbally and with their body language.

Box 4.1 Oversharing information with participants

George is studying for his MBA degree, and for his dissertation he decided to explore consumers' perceptions of eco labels. George was very happy as he managed to recruit seven participants for each of his four planned groups. He decided to audio record the sessions and transcribe them verbatim. During the first focus group participants kept asking George about the meaning of the various eco labels. Given that many eco labels include labelling jargon, he felt that there was a need to respond and explain the wording and/or the terminology. After a few clarifications the focus group dynamics changed and George became the centre of the group discussion, explaining certification vocabulary rather than initiating conversation around it. The main research question exploring consumer perceptions of eco labels was not addressed as participants reacted to the body language, the voice tone and the moderator's interpretation of each eco label. Phrases from George such as 'yes [smile], this one [label] is an official certification' influenced the views of the participants who wanted to agree with the moderator and be in line with official certifications rather than express their individual views and experiences, or be critical. After the second focus group and when no new information had emerged, a meeting was arranged with the dissertation supervisors for an update and feedback. During the meeting it became clear that discussing any type of jargon during the focus group was counterproductive. It was then suggested that a leaflet containing images of the displayed certifications and related information, from the official certification websites, could be provided to the participants a few days prior to the discussion. As a result, in the third focus group participants were keen to discuss the certifications in depth by further exploring the role of the various stakeholders, the label design, its location on the product packaging and they happily shared their own personal shopping stories. From this and the following focus group important marketing implications emerged which enabled George to make useful recommendations to companies and certification organisations. Based on George's recommendations a global fast moving consumer goods brand altered its labelling practice on their deodorant packaging. Thus, deciding what to say or share as a moderator can have a major effect on the nature of the collected data.

Moderating practical and conceptual topics

We find that encouraging participants to discuss conceptual issues and ideas is more challenging than asking them to comment on tangible elements such as product price or packaging. Our group discussions on internationalisation in higher education seemed to require much more creativity and flexibility in terms of moderation than our research on green products. In our project with graduate students on internationalisation we decided to use photo voice, which is a visual method where participants bring their photographs to discuss, as an additional layer in order to encourage discussion. Participants found it easier to relate to their own experiences by taking new photographs or using existing ones to express their views. We noticed that they were keen to share their stories and even memories. From this project we developed a conceptual model mapping essential elements of internationalisation in higher education from the students' own perspective.

Moderator multitasking

Moderators need to be able to focus on the group itself, on the participants and their responses, as well as their body language, and at the same time keep important notes without appearing disengaged to the group. This ability to mentally and physically multitask will prove useful during the discussion by actively engaging some less vocal participants and at the same time collecting many useful layers of data, such as body language, expressions, comments, interruptions and so on. If you do not yet have such skills, it might be worth considering an assistant moderator or co-facilitator to take notes of nonverbal behaviours or other dynamics that cannot be audio recorded. We find that our students are keen on this practice in their group dissertations as most of them are first-time adopters of the method and having two members of the team facilitates the process and the discussions.

What makes a good moderator?

Effective focus group moderators need to have or develop excellent communication skills that enable them to engage with a range of participants as well as with a research team or client company. Focus group projects might involve managers, employees, hospital patients, families, care home residents or minority groups, and the moderator needs to be able to communicate effectively with different participants. Many international researchers also find that communicating with focus group participants in a different language presents an additional challenge. This highlights the additional benefits of a well-prepared focus group agenda and a pilot study.

It is often the case that researchers have limited professional qualities like the ones reported in the literature. However, some individual characteristics are also vital for good discussion moderation. A good moderator is empathetic and able to understand the perspective of participants, is a good listener and sensitive towards participants, is respectful and insightful about participants, has good people skills and is creative, energetic and spontaneous (Krueger, 1998).

Greenbaum (2000) summarises the personal qualities of successful moderators, suggesting they are hardworking and able to work under stressful conditions and unusual working hours as participants are often only available in the evenings; self-motivating as they are usually the project leaders; self-confident and able to fulfil the requirements and challenges of the role; quick learners and able to absorb a great deal of information and become an 'instant expert' on the area of focus; friendly and engaging with participants as they are good listeners and encourage participation; and with a clear memory and focus which assist both the discussion but also the analysis.

Differences between interviewing and moderating

Researchers wishing to moderate their own focus groups need to be aware of the multifaceted moderator role which differs from the role of the one-to-one interviewer. We find that researchers often approach focus groups as they would one-to-one structured interviews. For instance, they place the participants in a circle and ask each participant the same question before proceeding to the next one and thus fail to capture the 'group element'. Krueger (1998) cautions that such practice may confuse the participants as to the intent of the inquiry. Having said that, we highlighted in Chapter 2 that the level of structure goes hand in hand with the philosophical underpinnings of a research topic and the research objectives. Consequently, focus groups informed by realist/objectivist assumptions which produce objective data can have a more structured approach, as opposed to the ones adopting an interpretive stance (Coule, 2013) with a less structured approach.

We have also observed anxious moderators focusing on the questions rather than on encouraging and motivating participation. Bloor et al. (2001) stress that the role of a moderator is not to control the group but to facilitate interaction as too much external control may distort it. Fortunately, most institutions are aware of the wide use of focus groups and offer seminars and workshops for first-time users of the method. Even if workshops are not available at the time of the project researchers can prepare by reading books, articles and watching online videos from reliable sources. In Box 4.2 we provide an example of the kind of preparatory work needed for a masters dissertation involving focus groups.

Box 4.2   Preparation for focus group moderation

Shuang is a masters student exploring consumer perceptions of themed brand stores for her dissertation. She wants to gain a deeper understanding of what consumers think and what type of associations they make with themed brand stores such as Hello Kitty coffee shops. Shuang has considered various qualitative methods and, reflecting on the research objectives, she decides to conduct focus groups. She starts reading articles and books by key authors in the field such as Barbour (2014), Greenbaum (2000), Krueger (1994), Morgan (1997) and Stewart and Shamdasani (2015) as a first step in familiarising herself with the method. However, after reading about the qualities expected in good moderators she feels intimidated and stressed about the role of the moderator. She decides not to give up and to do her best to prepare herself as she believes that her personal and social skills are very good. Shuang then decides to do an online search for videos on how to moderate focus groups. She finds that SAGE Research Methods Videos (http://methods.sagepub.com/Video) are very helpful. She then drafts questions for her discussion agenda and pilots this agenda with her peers and supervisors. Following this she feels both ready and excited to conduct her first focus group.

Finally, we would like to conclude that from all the professional and individual characteristics of the focus group moderator the most essential quality is ethical conduct. Researchers need to be aware of confidentiality issues attached to their moderating tasks and respect participants for their effort and time.

ETHICAL CONSIDERATIONS

Ethical concerns attached to primary data collection methods are in general terms quite similar. They involve confidentiality, data recording, safety and invasion of privacy. In this section we discuss the ethical concerns related to focus groups and how they can be managed during a research project.

Applying for ethical approval

Many institutions have raised the importance of ethics in research, making it the first step for research projects involving primary data collection methods. Researchers in higher education institutions are required to apply for ethical approval before commencing the data collection stage of their project. Anecdotal evidence suggests that this can be quite a stressful and time-consuming process that can last a few weeks depending on the sensitivity of the research theme and the methods employed. When applying for ethical approval, researchers need to be clear about their topic, sample, timeframe, methods, confidentiality, recordings, data handling, safety and process. They also need to provide supporting documentation for approval, such as the information sheet and consent form addressed to potential participants.

Information sheet

In the information sheet the researcher outlines basic information about their research project, expectations and the process as well as contact information of both the lead researcher and the institution. The project then becomes more transparent and the researcher more accessible to the participants, potentially making them more confident and willing to participate. The aim of the information sheet is to give an idea to potential participants of what to expect during the focus group discussions in simple everyday language and offer them the reassurance that this project has been approved by the institution's ethics committee. When completing this form it is important to remember the target group and use everyday language and keep away from any research jargon that will confuse potential participants. Each institution has their own ethics procedures and forms but many follow a generally similar process. In Box 4.3 we provide an example of a typical information sheet that we produced for a project on green consumption. In this information sheet we provide general information about the project and what will be expected from the participants. We include contact information for the lead researcher and the affiliated institution.

Box 4.3   A focus group information sheet

Green consumption and perceptions: a longitudinal study of consumers' perceptions of green products. Date [...]

You are being invited to take part in a research project. Before you decide it is important for you to understand why the research is being done and what it will involve. Please take time to read the following information carefully and discuss it with others if you wish. Ask us if there is anything that is not clear or if you would like more information. Take time to decide whether or not you wish to take part.

What is the project's purpose?

The aim of this project is to explore consumers' perceptions of green products. We are interested in finding out what motivates shopping for green products. We will use the findings to inform marketing strategies and green products.

Why have I been chosen?

You have been chosen because you indicated that you are responsible (partly or fully) for your household's shopping.

Do I have to take part?

It is up to you to decide whether or not to take part. If you do decide to take part you will be given this information sheet to keep and be asked to sign a consent form. You can still withdraw at any time without concern that there will be any negative outcome. You do not have to give a reason.

What will happen to me if I take part?

You will only have to be interviewed once for this project and it will take no longer than two hours. You will be part of a group discussion and share your views and stories with seven other consumers. During the interview you will be asked various questions regarding your shopping activities and your consumption. There will be no questions requiring special knowledge.

What are the possible benefits of taking part?

Whilst there are no immediate benefits to participating in this project, it is hoped that this work will shed some light onto consumers' perceptions of green products. In other words we will understand more of what motivates your shopping and what drives your consumption and perceptions overall and specifically towards green products.

Will my taking part in this project be recorded and kept confidential?

All the information that we collect about you during the course of the research will be kept strictly confidential by the research team. You will not be able to be identified in any reports or publications. The audio recordings will be used only for analysis. No other use will be made of them without your written permission, and no one outside the project will be allowed access to the original recordings.

How do I arrange participation?

We will be running focus groups in June, preferably in the evenings at 6:30pm. The dates are 15, 18, 28 and 30. If you wish to participate please email Panayiota at: *****

Thank you

Panayiota and Caroline

If a participant agrees to be part of the project the researcher can then provide the consent form which both will need to sign and keep a copy. It is essential that the consent form is signed before the focus group starts. In Box 4.4 we outline some standard questions that are part of this type of form.

Box 4.4   Example of a consent form

I confirm that I have read and understood the information sheet dated *[date]* explaining the research project and I have had the opportunity to ask questions about the project.

I understand that my participation is voluntary and that I am free to withdraw at any time without giving any reason and without there being any negative consequences.

I understand that my responses will be recorded and kept strictly confidential and are anonymous. I understand that my name will not be linked with the research materials, and I will not be identified or identifiable in the report or reports that result from the research.

I agree for the data collected from me to be used in future research.

I agree to take part in the above research project.

Name of participant   Date   Signature

Name of lead researcher   Date   Signature

Confidentiality and safety

In the case of focus groups there are specific concerns that need attention such as participants' confidentiality and the possibility of physical or psychological harm. For instance, with focus groups it is difficult, if not impossible, to promise absolute confidentiality to the participants as the researcher cannot control what each participant will do after the end of the discussions (Smith, 1995). Thus, it is recommended to address this issue at the start of the group where the moderator can acknowledge this and request confidentiality from the participants (Carey and Smith, 1992). The same applies in the case of personal harm when it becomes difficult to control individual reactions to personal stories and opinions. Nevertheless, it is the job of the moderator to address the issue prior to the start of the discussion, thus creating a fertile environment for shared experiences and individual views. Finally, recording the sessions needs to be clarified in writing prior to the start of the groups and thus needs a relevant section in both the information sheet and consent form.

Personal information

Participants provide personal information, both written and verbal, before, during and post focus group discussion. For instance, participants may complete a recruitment questionnaire offering personal information such as age, gender, education, family status and income. Participants are also invited to answer questions related to the research project. For instance, in the recruitment questionnaire for our project about product labelling in the UK we asked potential participants questions about their everyday shopping routine and their preferred retailer. Participants reveal personal information about their personality and behaviour which the researcher needs to protect and handle confidentially. We provide an example of a recruitment questionnaire in Chapter 3 (Box 3.4).

Recording the sessions

Audio recording is considered essential and it will help with transcription, translation and analysis. It is useful to explain why recording the session is important for the project. At the same time participants can be informed as to who will have access to the data. Typically this will be the researcher themselves and maybe supervisors. If the sessions are visually recorded, the participants need to agree, be aware of the recording process and understand its importance for the study. Video recording the sessions has many advantages, especially during analysis, but can also prohibit participation as it can be intrusive (Joseph et al., 2000). A digital recorder may be used, smart phones and tablets include recording applications and most online platforms (e.g. Skype) offer basic recording features as add-ons.

Research and ethics with sensitive populations

Researching with sensitive populations necessitates careful consideration as there are challenges in terms of ethical approval, literacy levels, use of appropriate language, inclusion of relevant materials, and timing (Tinson, 2009). Focus groups can be used with children providing the moderator has thought about the above issues and can maintain the children's attention for the desired duration. Examples of such research can be found in communication studies with Buckingham (1987) who looked at children as audiences for the UK soap opera *EastEnders*, and in social marketing with Peattie et al. (2001) who used focus groups to investigate children's understanding of sun safety in Australia. Both sets of authors were convinced that focus groups were an appropriate way of researching with children, but made it clear that maintaining children's attention to the topic of discussion was one of the major challenges to address. The focus group moderator has to be skilled in focusing and managing the group without being too prescriptive and must be adept at including all members, not just the vocal ones. With children in particular, it helps if the topic is relevant, interesting and accessible. In the UK, all researchers who would like to work with children must apply for a national disclosure service check as part of the ethics process, which can take time. Intention to work with other potentially vulnerable groups will also entail increased scrutiny by ethics reviewers and there may be additional questions to answer on the ethics application form.

THE FOCUS GROUP PROCESS

Once the ethics approval has been sought and granted, the pilot study has been completed and the researcher has made the necessary adjustments to the discussion agenda, the most exciting part of the research commences. In Figure 4.1 we have mapped the main activities the researcher will go through on the day of the focus group.

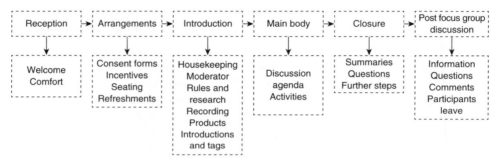

Figure 4.1   The focus group process

Reception

Overall, a warm welcome from the moderator and an exchange of a few general pleasantries can relax the participants and make them feel at ease.

Arrangements

After greeting participants a few arrangements need to be made. First the moderator gives the consent forms to the participants to sign if this has not already been done. At the same time participants sign for and receive the agreed incentives (if applicable). Following this, they are shown to their chairs and offered some refreshments. The seating arrangements should encourage participation and every participant should be able to make eye contact with the other participants and the moderator.

Introduction

At this stage all the respondents have had time to relax, exchange some basic information, sign the forms and prepare for the discussion. The moderator goes through some basic housekeeping information like location of cloakrooms, fire exits and potential alarms. Following this the moderator may, providing permission has been granted, start recording the session. It is advisable to run through some basic rules and make clear to all the respondents that there are no right or wrong answers and that every opinion is valued. One usual practice we adopt for our focus groups is to have name tags for our participants. The participants can introduce themselves by sharing something personal and attach the name tag to their clothing.

Main body of discussion

This is where the main discussion begins with the moderator starting with some ice breaker questions followed by introductory questions. At this point the attention falls on covering the discussion agenda with key questions and activities.

Closure

Closing the discussion with a few summary questions indicates that the key themes have been covered and that the time has come to end the discussion. What works well at this stage is to offer the opportunity to each participant to summarise some basic points or close with some remarks, recommendations or final statements. This is also a chance for the moderator to invite questions from participants and to inform them of the next steps. After the final remarks and questions the moderator can end the discussion and thank the participants.

Post focus group discussion activities

When the focus group is over participants may informally discuss their opinions that were not expressed during the session as well as their opinions about the session itself. The less talkative participants may feel happier sharing their views if any dominant participants have left the venue. Morgan (1997) suggests this discussion can be recorded, but participants would need to be fully aware that the recorder is still running. A debriefing session with the moderator and co-facilitator, if applicable, can be done via note taking, or an additional tape recording.

Practitioners use a metaphor for the entire process which feeds back to Tuckman's (1964) model of group development. To get an idea of how a professional moderator views the focus group process we asked a practitioner from a marketing research agency. Professional moderators see the focus group as having five stages: forming, with individuals seeking inclusion in the discussion; storming, power and control, which provide evidence of interaction; norming, which indicates feeling part of the group; performing, which involves tasks and activities; and finally mourning, time to let go and leave.

Moderating difficult situations

It is very common for the moderator to encounter problems during the group discussion. These can be either technical problems or participant problems. Researchers are reminded to check their recording equipment and ensure that it is fully charged and has enough recording space. The most common problems in a focus group setting, however, come from participants. Krueger (1998) has grouped these problematic cases of participants into six categories:

- Experts and influentials are participants who have experience of the topic, a relevant background or have focus group experience and can inhibit others in the group. The moderator can acknowledge their experience and ask the rest of the group to contribute their opinion.
- Dominant talkers are participants who consider themselves experts and dominate the discussion. The moderator can avoid eye contact and can encourage participation from the rest of the group.
- Disruptive participants exhibit disruptive behaviour. The moderator can remind the participant of the rules and if the behaviour remains the same, ask the person to leave the discussion.
- Ramblers and wanderers are chatty participants who take their time in making a point. The moderator should cease eye contact or ask a question as soon as the participant pauses.
- Quiet and shy participants speak very little. The moderator can encourage these participants to voice an opinion by having frequent eye contact or calling their name.
- Inattentive participants have a hard time staying focused and on topic. The moderator may need to repeat the question or even write it down.

No matter how well you have planned your focus group research, you should be prepared for surprises. The types of participants described above are very common in focus groups, especially the shy and dominant ones, and you need to have a few strategies in hand to deal with such participants.

AFTER THE GROUP: DEALING WITH FORMS AND DATA

After the end of the focus group discussions, the moderator needs to ensure that the recordings, the consent forms and the rest of the materials are safely stored on a PC and/or in a locked cabinet which only the researcher can access. It is highly recommended to back up the files to avoid any loss of data. Alternatively, storing data files online (e.g. on Google Drive, OneDrive, or Dropbox) with a strong passcode is another way of securing them and allowing access to supervisors if appropriate.

Transcription

Researchers generate textual materials from their primary data to facilitate the analysis and reporting process. This usually happens by transcribing the audio or video recordings, as textual formats provide easier ways of managing, searching and retrieving data (Silver and Lewins, 2014). Transcribing is time consuming but a recognisable route to data familiarisation, analysis and reporting. Usually one hour of audio tape recording equals approximately seven hours of transcription.

Many authors have acknowledged the importance of 'verbatim' transcriptions of the interview or focus group recordings. As such the conventional understanding of transcription error, the difference between written records (transcripts) and audio tape recordings, could be minimised. Poland (1995) emphasises the importance of these verbatim accounts of what transpired in the focus group, especially in terms of establishing trustworthiness and rigour in qualitative research, while acknowledging that at best they are partial records and accounts of a wider interaction and experience. This applies especially to focus groups where body language, the tone of the voices, the pauses and reactions and interactions are a major source of data generation and analysis. Transcribing verbatim the tapes brings back the 'feel' of the group and aids recollection of the group participants. This way quotes are assigned to the appropriate participant. In the case of focus groups where participants talk simultaneously, this is a great challenge. An easy trick to remember is to ask participants to share their name and a short introduction about themselves. This way the transcriber can make the connection between names and voices. Another way to facilitate this process is to repeat the name of the participant: 'So, Lisa, you mentioned that...'. It is helpful to transcribe focus group data as soon as possible, while the memory of the discussion is still fresh. Of course not all audio recordings need to be transcribed word by word. In research situations pressured by time or which involve fairly mundane issues researchers can rely on notes or the recordings instead of full transcripts. In this case, summary transcriptions may be used. For instance, in one of our projects we explored purchase behaviour of consumers in Paris. The results were quite unexpected at the time and French consumers seemed to be very knowledgeable about green products. Our client organisation insisted on repeating the groups in another city to see if this surprisingly high interest in green consumption was evident elsewhere. We decided to conduct a number of groups in Bordeaux. After a few groups we could report similar reactions and perceptions between consumers in the two cities. In the case of Paris the transcriptions were verbatim and, as can be seen in Box 4.5, essential observational information was included as well as the speaker identification. In the case of Bordeaux we conducted a summary transcription as we wanted to reflect on the findings in Paris.

Box 4.5   Examples of verbatim and summary transcriptions

Verbatim transcription in Paris on green consumption behaviour

Moderator: Can you check the information on this product [brand F] and tell me what you think?

S: I am suspicious about that one! I do not trust it much...

D: Me neither!

[*Silence for a few seconds*]

[*Participants look at the products for a few seconds*]

[*D makes a start and picks up product 5. The rest follow*]

[*Silence*]

[*They explore the product packaging of brands I, C, F, G*]

[*S and D discuss the type of information they found on brand F and the rest follow*]

[*They all seem surprised with the amount of information*]

[*Men ask the moderator about the sustainability labels on brands I and C*]

[*Women are more focused on the product information, such as ingredients*]

M: We do not pay that much attention to that sort of information. Once I bought a perfume from an airplane on my way back home. I tried it on and a few hours later the smell had gone!

[Moderator's note: M made an association between the topic of discussion and the duration of a perfume bought on-board]

Summary transcription in Bordeaux on green consumption behaviour

Moderator: Can you check the information on this product [brand F] and tell me what you think?

I do not understand

I don't trust

Limited information

[*Limited understanding of information*]

Including observational data that were obtained during the discussions along with the quotes stressing important points, the tone of the voice, a pause, expressions of intensity or humour are beneficial for the analysis stage. As Stewart and Shamdasani (2015) mention, the moderator or an observer may be able to add further information, based on group observations and interactions, that is not apparent from the text. As seen in Box 4.5, in the case of a verbatim approach the observational data included has added an important layer for the subsequent analysis. Thus, in the same example the reaction of participants when they explore the products may be interpreted as follows: participants show interest and/or curiosity in labelling; participants 'discover' a range of product labelling practices; participants are not familiar with all the types of labelling on products; there are differences between female and male participants.

Krueger (1998) offers important advice to researchers who are not transcribing their own recordings. He stresses the importance of verifying the transcripts and making sure that they accurately reflect the recording. In our research on internationalisation in higher education we conducted a study with overseas students and due to time pressure we had the recordings transcribed by a professional transcriber. When we read the transcriptions we realised that many parts of the discussion were missing and had been replaced by the indication: [*inaud 7.51*]. This meant that the transcriber could not make sense of the discussion around a specific time. We also realised that the transcriber did not assign the correct pseudonyms to our participants and was not familiar with the accents of our international group members. We decided to complete the missing sections ourselves by listening to the discussions several times.

Issues that may affect the transcription process include the recording equipment, the quality of the recording, the location of the discussions, participants engaging in small talk in pairs and in low voices around the table and, most of all, participants expressing their views simultaneously which is very common in group situations. The transcription process can be facilitated by using transcription technology. Researchers can acquire professional digital transcription kits that include a foot pedal, a stereo handset for hands-free operation and related software. However, there are other options available online such as TranscriberAG, ExpressScribe and F4/F5, which perform a similar role. The idea behind these systems is to allow the transcriber to adjust the speed of the tape in order to capture the discussion word by word. They also allow insertion of speaker identifiers in a discussion. Silver and Lewins (2014) point out that with some of the transcription packages the transcript can remain linked to the associated media file (audio or video), which 'enables the subsequent analysis of the audio/video file concurrently with the written version' (p. 99). For instance, NVivo incorporates a transcription table alongside a video file, thus allowing the researcher to explore both the written text and the audio-visual data.

Translation

Focus groups are often used in cross-cultural research but this has certain challenges. Barbour and Kitzinger (1998) point out the limitations and methodological implications and argue that focus groups may be inappropriate for use in cross-cultural research unless specific attention is given to the cultural context. Being familiar with the cultural context offers the researcher a notable advantage in all stages of the focus group. In our cross-cultural research on sustainable consumption we conducted focus groups with consumers in Greece, the UK, France and Sweden. We found that participants responded in a different manner in each country during the discussions. For instance, the empty nesters (parents whose children had left home) in Greece expressed their opinions quite passionately and loudly, and in many cases simultaneously, whereas their counterparts in Sweden mainly took turns, politely expressing their opinions. In France consumers focused on existing trends and aesthetics whereas in the UK they focused more on government initiatives and policy. All participants agreed that culture plays an important part in their behaviour and noted that consumers in Nordic countries are more environmentally conscious than other Europeans. Being aware of these cultural characteristics prompted us to go beyond generally accepted assumptions (even stereotypes) about environmental sensitisation of various countries to look more closely into associations with sustainable consumption, such as facilitators, challenges and opportunities in each country. These findings informed our study in terms of government support, local initiatives and policy.

Language itself presents a considerable challenge, giving qualitative research an additional layer of complexity. In the same project on sustainability we ran the groups in the participants' native language as it is believed to be advantageous: Barbour (2007) mentions that participants using their first language are more spontaneous during discussions, which generates much richer data. Jagosh and Boudreau (2009) point out that the literature on translation theory originates from the quantitative fields for application of surveys and other methods across multilingual settings. In other words, researchers in quantitative studies develop a culturally equivalent research instrument which is psychometrically tested after translation (Barbour, 2007). However, as Esposito (2001) points out, these quantitative instruments are frozen in time compared to qualitative ones where researchers seek to reflect a changing social context. This adds a level of complexity in translation considerations for focus groups as researchers not fluent in participants' language must use a professional translator and/or interpreter and need to ensure methodological rigour (Esposito, 2001).

A popular method of dealing with translation is the back-translation technique (Brislin, 1970), in which the research instrument is written in the source language, then translated to the required language and then translated back to the source language. The researcher then analyses the three versions and pilots the result to test consistency. Of course the method is not without its criticisms (Larkin et al., 2007) as it makes assumptions that the research is unaffected by language and the same meanings can be found in various languages. A meaning-based rather than word-based translation is seen as a better option as in some cases literal translation may convey negative or inappropriate meanings. Culley et al. (2007) discussed methodological challenges in their study of provision of infertility services to south Asian communities in three English cities. They noticed that when translating the word 'infertility' some terms could not be used as they had negative connotations, as a literal translation of the word came close to the word 'barren' in English (Culley et al., 2007). Finally, Temple and Young (2004) call for a social constructionist approach to the translation process as the translator is seen as an active producer of knowledge. Thus, researchers translating their discussion agendas and their transcripts need to be aware of this additional layer of complexity and address methodological challenges systematically (Squires, 2009).

SUMMARY

In this chapter, we have drawn attention to the role of the moderator and the skills required to moderate a focus group. We emphasised that ethical considerations play a crucial role in how the researcher moderates the focus group, with practical steps to take before, during and after the process. We examined the ordering of questions and the different dynamics as the focus group gets underway, with strategies on how to deal with tricky participants. Issues around transcription and translation as informed by cross-cultural research were also addressed.

In the next chapter, we provide examples from different areas of business and management research which have used focus groups to collect data. These examples come from published studies and cover a range of focus group practice, from using focus groups as a stand-alone method, to using them in a mixed methods inquiry and so on. The examples demonstrate how focus groups have been integrated with the specific research aims and objectives of each study, and how the focus groups have been used according to structure and purpose.

5

EXAMPLES OF FOCUS GROUPS

INTRODUCTION

In this chapter we provide examples of how focus groups have been used in research in business and management literature. In reflecting the nature of research that tends to employ focus groups as a method, there will be an emphasis on studies from the marketing discipline, as this is where we find much of the published work, yet we can see how focus groups have been used in other domains too, such as logistics, information systems and organisational behaviour. The different types of focus group structure presented earlier in Table 2.1 are used as a framework for the following discussion, and we also include examples of how focus groups are used in different research designs, such as stand-alone, mixed methods, and multi-methods.

UNSTRUCTURED FOCUS GROUPS

With this kind of focus group, the aim is to explore a new topic for research, or to gather general background information about a topic. Here, the researchers may not know what kinds of questions are appropriate, or what kind of language to use, and would like to hear participants speaking in their own words. Thus, the level of structure may be understated compared to focus groups with a different aim. We look at two examples of exploratory focus group research below.

Unstructured focus groups: exploratory

The first example of an exploratory focus group can be found in Knittel et al. (2016) who examined brand avoidance in Generation Y consumers. Generation Y represents adults who were born between the early 1980s to around the middle 1990s, although some definitions offer a wider range of years to encompass the whole of the 1980s and 1990s (Oxford Dictionary, 2016). Knittel et al. suggested that researchers have traditionally focused on the positive relationship between consumers and brands, but increasingly, consumers are consciously avoiding brands – for Generation Y, this avoidance is little understood. Therefore, an exploratory design was chosen due to the limited pre-existing research on this subject, as well as the desire to explore brand avoidance in more detail and in a different setting from previous research. Thus, the authors proposed a multi-methods design, starting with focus groups which they justified by noting that they are 'especially useful in exploratory research where little is known about the phenomenon' (2016: 33). Using personal contacts and a flyer, they recruited 18 participants aged between 23 and 32 years, from Germany, Finland, Slovakia, Bulgaria, Poland and Estonia. The range of countries reflected the student nature of the participants, all of whom were enrolled in various courses at Jönköping University in Sweden. The focus groups were run by a moderator with the aid of a guideline comprising questions and follow-up probes, and a researcher also observed and took notes. In addition, the discussions were audio recorded. The focus group participants were not informed about the topic of discussion in advance, but were simply told that the discussion would be about buying goods and consumption; they were therefore all eligible to take part. In this multi-methods design, the authors then undertook individual unstructured interviews with four of the focus group participants to investigate in further detail certain issues arising from the group discussions. These four were selected based on the judgement of the researchers with agreement from the participants. The transcribed data were analysed by searching for recurring themes and ideas which resonated with brand avoidance and coded using CAQDAS (Computer Aided Qualitative Data Analysis Software), resulting in five broad motives and several sub-motives for brand avoidance, including a new type of brand avoidance, which the authors termed 'advertising avoidance'. Knittel et al. illustrated these motives with the aid of verbatim quotes from the transcribed focus groups, producing a rich account. Hence, the focus groups in this study were used to generate evidence to enable the authors to propose an answer to their original research question of why Generation Y consumers avoid brands.

The second example of an exploratory focus group design can be found in a study by Pendry et al. (2012). This was an initial investigation into attitudes around the use of traditional cloth nappies (or diapers) versus disposable nappies and is informative in the way the 11 focus groups were organised. The authors' stated aim was to understand what motivated parents to choose traditional or disposable styles, within a context of promoting environmentally friendly parenting. Little previous research existed and Pendry et al. drew upon general research around the environmental impact of products and environmental psychology to inform their study. All the 35 participants were female, 32 had at least one child under three years of age, and three were expecting their first child. They were approached mainly via informal means such as local toddler groups, friends, word-of-mouth and online discussion forums. The group size ranged from two to eight participants with the exception of one instance where a participant was interviewed alone (the other members did not turn up). The authors constructed the focus groups according to whether the participant was a cloth or disposable nappy user, keeping the two separate. There was also use of both face-to-face and online focus groups, which followed the same questioning format. The authors constructed a general topic guide consisting of seven themes: experience of use, economic factors, health factors, knowledge of alternatives, situational factors, being green and identity, which they deemed flexible enough to allow further exploration during the focus groups. The face-to-face groups, which lasted for approximately 90 minutes with a short break halfway through, were audio recorded and fully transcribed. The online groups, which also took around 90 minutes, did not require transcription as the full text was available once the sessions were finished. All groups were moderated by one of the authors. The authors deliberated whether it would be possible to merge the data from the two sources as they noted that the differences in format may have led to a loss of dynamics and non-verbal input in the online groups. They found that the online focus group participants contributed shorter comments compared to those in the face-to-face groups, but on implementation of the thematic analysis, they concluded that the data were equally rich and overlap in terms of emerging themes was high enough to warrant merging the data. Pendry et al. (2012) also noted that because their research was exploratory in nature, there were no a priori theoretical questions to guide their coding process. Hence, their approach to analysis was data driven rather than theory driven. This resulted in a thematic map based on push/pull factors around initial choice and continuation of use of either cloth or disposable nappies. The authors were then able to look at these factors in terms of marketing solutions for increasing future demand for traditional cloth nappies. As the first study to explore this specific topic, the authors used the focus group data to surface the complexities around environmental parenting and to address their initial aim to understand parental attitudes and decisions around this choice. Thus, this study is an example of the use of focus groups, both face to face and online, as a single method in an exploratory design.

SEMI-STRUCTURED FOCUS GROUPS

Semi-structured focus groups: theory development

The first semi-structured focus group presented in Table 2.1 is designed to generate data to inform theory development. In this kind of design, there will be existing theory or theories to draw upon which the study aims to contribute to or expand. It may be that previous studies have taken a particular philosophical approach, such as positivism, engaging with quantitative methods and analysis, and there is merit in taking a more interpretive and qualitative approach. For example, the work of Chan et al. (2013), in which they sought greater insights into how adolescents in Hong Kong respond to celebrity endorsers, justified the adoption of focus groups in a field previously dominated by surveys.

An example of this focus group design can be found in Newman and Oates (2014) who used family focus groups to investigate how parents mediate food marketing communications aimed at children. The three research questions for their study were: what food marketing messages do parents regard as necessitating mediation; what forms of mediation do they use to counter food marketing messages; and have newer forms of food marketing communications affected parental mediation practices? In a context of the integration of marketing communications, and the constant development of digital and social media channels, the authors were keen to see how families constructed their individual and shared meanings around food and food marketing and so the inclusion of both parents and children in the research process was regarded as fundamental to the study. To achieve this, focus groups were chosen as the most suitable method, and the authors explained this decision and compared the kinds of data they could have gathered with a more quantitative approach. They also provided an account of how the families were approached, as it can be a challenging task to find participants for such research. The authors used a combination of contacting families known to them, snowballing to other families and advertising for research participants on local family forum websites. All these activities received ethical approval from the authors' university ethics committee.

The focus groups were run with the aid of prompts. Newman and Oates (2014) prepared visual materials to use in the focus groups, which allowed even the youngest children (aged five) to indicate their recognition of the various marketing communications. All the focus groups were moderated by the first author, who made the groups feel informal and relaxed by wherever possible sitting on the same level as the children in the family, which often meant sitting on the floor. The discussions began with general questions aimed at the parents to gather background information and then more specific questions were posed, which included the whole family. (See Chapter 3 where we discuss the formatting of questions in detail.) Having both parents and children present facilitated a very rich set of data because the parents and children were often surprised at what the other said, and so there were questions between the participants, as well as much laughter and some denial of what happened during family food shopping trips and eating habits. From this data, the authors produced 261 pages of full transcripts, which were then analysed using the four interactive stages of Miles et al. (2014). This detailed and iterative process of analysis, which involves data collection, data reduction, data display and drawing conclusions, enabled the authors to address their three research questions and to develop an extension to existing mediation theory. They concluded by proposing a new category of parental mediation to cover food marketing communications encountered outside the home environment. Hence, the authors demonstrate how focus groups can be used to build theory.

A second example of the semi-structured focus group designed to develop theory is illustrated in an article by Oates et al. (2003). Here, the authors were concerned with exploring how children understand television advertising and they expressed a desire to move away from the more usual quantitative approach which had largely dominated the literature throughout the previous decades. The authors felt that a more nuanced approach to what we mean by 'understanding' advertising was needed, particularly in the light of mixed results about the age of understanding from earlier research. They decided to use focus groups as the only method of data collection (we discuss the ethical issues around focus groups with child participants in Chapter 4).

In Oates et al.'s (2003) study, 40 focus groups were carried out with a total of 182 schoolchildren ranging in age from 5 to 10 years. The number of focus groups in this study was noticeably higher than in most studies, and we would not advocate aiming for 40 groups in dissertation projects. However, this example usefully serves to highlight the characteristics of using focus groups with even very young children. For example, as appropriate for this age range, the focus groups were shorter in time than one would expect with adults, and Oates et al. (2003) noted that the average length of a group with the five and six year olds (the youngest participants) was around nine minutes. For the older children, aged between nine and ten years, the groups lasted on average for 10.5 minutes. The groups were also small, with only four or five children in each one. Prior to the data collection, the authors first identified five related topic areas from the literature on children's understanding of advertising and clustered questions around these, using them to organise the flow of the focus groups. These topics included: the role of television advertisements, attitudes towards them, their location, characteristics and source. All the groups were moderated by the same person, who was skilled at working with children in the classroom. The focus groups were audio recorded and fully transcribed. From analysis of these transcripts and the initial five topics, the authors identified three overall themes which emerged from the data, and which extended the theory of how children understand television advertising. They proposed that understanding should be disengaged from its current focus purely on age to incorporate personal experience, economic understanding and a sense of time. They were able to use the focus group data to widen the debate to incorporate these three additional criteria which explained why previous studies had found inconsistent and mixed results in understanding. The authors concluded that their qualitative methodological approach enabled a unique perspective to be surfaced around children's understanding of television advertising.

The two examples outlined above show the variety of focus group research within the semi-structured theory building design. Even though the examples share certain common features, we can see how differently the focus groups are conceived and run according to the aim of each project.

Semi-structured focus groups: impression gathering

The second focus group design under semi-structured focus groups is that of impression gathering, which can be applied to products, brands, services or organisations. With this aim, researchers seek to explore how a particular phenomenon is received by participants. This might be part of a wider project, and be related to a specific purpose, for example to explore initial impressions of employees with the goal of introducing change into their workplace. We illustrate this design with an example from the organisational studies literature, where Stiles (2004) used focus groups to elicit and explore the impressions that academics, professional services staff, students and the wider business community have of business schools in universities in Canada and the UK. The study design took a multi-methods approach with 76 face-to-face interviews followed by 18 focus groups. In the interviews, participants were asked to draw their organisation as a personality (as a human figure) and to offer a verbal interpretation of this drawing to the interviewer. A selection of five of these drawings together with their interpretation was then taken to the focus groups to explore whether a particular image captured what the focus group participants considered to offer the best impression of their business school. The ensuing discussion around which picture should be chosen, including the rationales for consensus and disagreement, was fully recorded on video. The focus groups were then asked by the moderator to produce a composite drawing of their own, again with verbal commentary. The full transcripts were analysed using a discourse analysis approach, defined by Stiles as the process of examining the transcribed texts for consistencies (more than one participant mentions the same thing) and variabilities (appearance of a unique perception in the text). Because all the pictures were accompanied by their description, there was no need for the researcher to undertake a separate interpretation of the images themselves. Stiles suggested that by using such pictorial techniques, it was possible to produce rich insights which can enhance understanding, surfacing latent tensions via the exercise of identifying an organisational personality. In this way, the focus groups revealed unhappiness with management leadership styles, seen as uncommunicative, abrasive and distant. This was a common theme across both countries in the study. When data were gathered again after two years, using the same methods but this time only in the Canadian business school, analysis showed a cautiously optimistic picture due to the appointment of a new leader in the organisation. Stiles used the research to develop strategic objectives for each institution in the study yet acknowledged that even without this higher goal, the research would still have been useful in enhancing a broad understanding of organisational identity. Stiles' example demonstrates the use of focus groups in a multi-methods design to gather impressions of organisations from various stakeholders.

A second example of a focus group designed to gather impressions can be found in the work of Sohail and Shaikh (2004). In this study, the authors were keen to examine student impressions of service quality in higher education. Specifically, the authors wanted to gain insights into the dimensions used by students to assess what components of the delivery process are considered to be important. In a mixed methods research design, the authors chose to run a focus group first, to aid the development of a survey instrument. Thus the study was structured in such a way as to privilege a quantitative outcome. After a review of the service quality literature, a list of critical variables that influence student evaluations of service quality was identified, and this list was taken to a focus group of 12 students. The participants were briefed about the purpose of the focus group and shown the list. They were asked to select and consider the variables that they identified as important when assessing service quality. From the long list of variables, participants selected 32 through a process of discussion and elimination. The focus group lasted for approximately two hours and was run by a moderator with two observers present. In this research design, the inclusion of the focus group was clearly intended to inform the next stage – the development of a questionnaire. Consequently, a 32-item questionnaire based on the focus group outcome was constructed and distributed to a random sample of business students, generating 310 responses. These responses were analysed using factor analysis, which produced six factors that influence students' impressions of service quality, the main one being contact personnel. Thus, based on the initial focus group and the quantitative questionnaire, Sohail and Shaikh (2004) suggested that managers should work more closely with faculty and administrative personnel, as this makes a significant contribution to students' impressions of the college. This study is an illustration of using a focus group as a precursor to designing and implementing a quantitative survey with an overall aim of impression gathering.

Semi-structured focus groups: diagnostic

The next use of focus groups identified in Table 2.1 is that of the diagnostic method (i.e. to examine a new product or service with the aim of identifying or diagnosing problems or success factors). This kind of research is often found in the marketing practitioner literature, for example the boxed cake mix scenario we described in Chapter 2 (Morgan, 1998).

This use of focus groups can also be seen in the academic literature. For example, as part of a larger study which was developed to test a dual innovation in wine geotraceability and authentication, Cochoy (2015) described how four focus groups were used to investigate the idea of the consumer as part of a co-production process. By using the innovative and interactive labelling system on wine bottles as a stimulus, Cochoy examined both the viability of the new labelling itself (the diagnostic element of the focus groups) and how it can inform theoretical notions of the working consumer – in other words, investigating the activity or work that consumers have to perform to use such labels. Cochoy (2015: 141) deliberately chose focus groups as the single method with which to probe this topic, suggesting that they 'provide better access to the actual dynamics of ordinary consumption than the conduct of individual interviews, which are more detached from the circumstances of practice'. Participants for one of the focus groups were carefully selected according to their consumption of wine (wine amateurs); another group was made up of young professionals who use smartphones (technophiles). The remaining two groups consisted of 'ordinary' people, making a total of 28 participants. The groups were moderated by the researchers working on the project and recorded. With the inclusion of verbatim discussion excerpts from the groups, Cochoy illustrated how painstaking it was for participants to use the prototype device and the problems they experienced in attempting to scan the labels. The actions of the participants such as moving the bottles, adjusting their smartphones, and attempting to click through to the correct website, were fully described along with the accompanying conversations, providing insight into how participants attempted to work with the innovation, and how most of them ultimately failed to complete the first step of accessing the website. Each group of participants had different concerns and difficulties.

So, from a diagnostic perspective, the focus groups revealed the extent to which the innovation presented many difficulties, and how it was experienced by the different groups of users. From a more theoretical perspective, Cochoy used the data to argue that the harder participants had to work at the desired activity, the less likely they were to become actual consumers, at least in this case of the prototype labelling device. He concluded that for such a device to be successful, it would have to minimise the work of the consumer. Thus, focus groups were used effectively to diagnose the many problems with this particular innovation, and how it might be improved.

A second example of the diagnostic focus group design comes from the library management literature, with a study by Crowley et al. (2002). They were interested to see how a university's new library web interface was received by a wide variety of users, including undergraduates, postgraduates, academic staff, teaching staff and library faculty. The new interface had been designed to make finding information much easier but after its launch in the university, library staff noticed patrons having difficulty in using the search facility. They decided to carry out research with users to diagnose the problems with the new service. The authors chose to use focus groups because they are 'extremely useful for exploring how patrons will respond to a new idea, service or product' (p.206) and they based their study on this method alone. The authors recruited 26 participants to take part in seven focus groups, with each group comprising a specific set of users, such as undergraduate students. For each group, the moderator followed a similar format with the use of a question guide (protocol) consisting of three main areas. To begin, the moderator asked participants to think about the way they used the library to conduct research, specifically in terms of available electronic resources. Ten sub-questions expanded on this initial theme. Second, the moderator suggested narrowing the focus of the discussion to the library's web page, with five more sub-questions to probe this area.

Third, participants were asked to think about how the library marketed its electronic resources, with three specific sub-questions to expand this area. Finally, the moderator asked for any general comments or questions from the group. All the groups were recorded and the recordings fully transcribed. The authors described their approach to analysis as rooted in grounded theory, where theory is driven by the data. They undertook a detailed analysis, comparing across the groups to organise the data into emerging themes, in a process they called concept mapping. Through this activity, they identified five themes which related to the problems experienced by users: a need for more research portals; access to research resources; user skill and knowledge; awareness of resources; and general attitudes towards libraries and their services. Crowley et al. illustrated each point with verbatim quotes from the participants. They concluded by noting that the insights gained from these focus groups would enable the library web team to create a more intuitive interface. They also noted that by talking with many different users, and comparing data across the focus groups, a divide was observable between more and less experienced participants, and so the possibility of a two-tier interface (advanced and basic) was suggested. Thus, Crowley et al.'s study demonstrates how using focus groups can lead to diagnosing problems with a service, and at the same time can enable the researchers to gather insights into how that service might be improved.

Semi-structured focus groups: explanatory

The fourth focus group design we have included under semi-structured designs is that of the explanatory focus group, used to interpret findings from a previous and/or related survey. Here, the researcher seeks to understand further the phenomenon which is being studied. For example, Daymon and Holloway (2011) recounted a survey result which showed 52 per cent of respondents found it too much trouble to complain about poor customer service. Subsequent focus group research was able to explain this statistic in terms of the scepticism held by participants about how seriously organisations respond to such complaints. In a different field, Bernon and Cullen (2007) reported how they used a focus group at the end of a study into reverse logistics to help them compare earlier research findings from case studies and a postal survey. They noted that data obtained in the focus group provided them with additional insights about reverse logistics processes.

In our first example Shammas (2017) reported on how she followed up a quantitative survey she had first conducted in 2007. The survey originally addressed whether Arab and Muslim community college students perceive a high level of discrimination against them by other students, faculty, and/or administration. The original survey findings had been inconsistent and ambiguous, and Shammas suspected there may have been a problem in the perceived discrimination measure or perhaps students were underreporting discrimination on campus. To address this uncertainty, the author decided to use a qualitative approach to aid further understanding of these previous results, and to gain direct access to the different views of this student population. She employed a sequential explanatory mixed methods design in which a quantitative data analysis preceded the qualitative data collection. The qualitative findings then served to make meaning of the quantitative results. For the qualitative phase Shammas recruited 16 community college students to participate in three focus groups to explore if they are reticent to disclose or possibly deny feelings of personal or group discrimination in the college. To guide the focus groups, she developed a list of research questions which explicitly related to the survey, so for example the first three research questions were constructed to elaborate on the nine survey items corresponding to perceived discrimination and the campus climate. All the groups were audio recorded and transcribed, and content analysed by two researchers. Whilst the survey results and focus group findings did not differ markedly from each other, the focus group participants produced rich narratives, illuminating why ethnic minorities might conceal or underreport incidents of discrimination. Thus, the quantitative outcomes were further explored and understood with the aid of the focus group discussions.

A second study utilising an explanatory focus group design can be found in an article by Spanjaard et al. (2014) who investigated emotions in supermarket shopping behaviour. They suggested that there are underlying psychological processes that shape shopping behaviour in ways consumers are not aware of and so cannot report in conventional survey methods, and which are not visible in traditional shopping observation studies. Because of this, Spanjaard and her colleagues considered a mixed methods and integrated design which began with conducting a quantitative survey to provide a snapshot of grocery buying activities, and then followed with detailed qualitative research to uncover some of the reasons behind the behaviour identified by the survey. The authors judged that a survey alone was inadequate to address any arising issues in sufficient detail and so a mixed methods approach, with specific emphasis on qualitative outcomes, was chosen. The resulting design used multiple techniques where the results of one method fed into the design of the next. The first qualitative method to follow the survey was a focus group, the structure of which was directly informed by the survey results. The survey performed two functions – one was to provide insights which were then taken up in the focus group and explored in more depth, and the other was to provide participants for the focus group itself. A single focus group with ten participants was held to provide a general understanding of consumers' reflections on how they make grocery purchasing decisions, and to guide development of a later stage of individual in-depth interviews. For example, the authors reported that an unexpected finding from the focus group was the important but highly ambiguous notion of quality. Quality issues were mentioned frequently and seen to be central to participants' concerns around grocery shopping, but they found it difficult to articulate what they meant by the term. Accordingly, the subsequent individual interviews included questions on the nature and role of quality. Other insights emerging from the focus group also provided input for the ensuing research design with the resulting interview protocol emphasising the need to consider the importance and influence of (in)tangible aspects and the interactions within and between them. For example, of particular relevance was the presence of trust as a mechanism in brand decision-making. Following the focus group, the authors proceeded to use videographic observation, in-depth interviews and diaries, providing opportunities for participants to supply a much more holistic picture of why they make the choices they do in the supermarket context. Spanjaard et al. (2014) also pointed out that further value comes from interrelating these various data forms to create synergy of insight. They concluded that application of the combined research methods allowed insights that any one, or even two, techniques may not have achieved. Whilst surveys will most certainly capture simple behavioural and attitudinal responses to the retail environment, they suggested that if used in conjunction with qualitative methods, further insights will surface about why certain brands are chosen in the grocery store.

ADDITIONAL DESIGNS FOR FOCUS GROUP RESEARCH

There are some additional ways of designing focus groups that we have not covered in this chapter, as they are not very common and perhaps out of the general scope of a dissertation project but you may come across these in your literature reviews. For example, Bill and Olaison (2009) propose something they call an 'indirect semi-focused group' in which they combine the traditional focus group setting with a piece of role-play. They suggest this approach enables 'participants to act and talk as if they were dealing with a real task, rather than merely narrating their experience to the researchers' (p.24). Initially conceived as a means of exploring the rationale behind owner-managers' decisions to participate in support programmes, Bill and Olaison set up a carefully designed process which involved inviting five owners of small and medium-sized enterprises (SMEs) to a focus group (without revealing the purpose of the group). Once they arrived, the participants were given time to socialise over coffee to create a context for the subsequent role play. Next, the researchers introduced the role play scenario of a board meeting to select a new chief executive officer (CEO) for a fictitious company, complete with fictitious CVs, all prepared in advance. The participants then engaged in the role play without any input from the researchers. The moderator did not intervene until the 'board meeting' was closed and then they initiated a discussion of what had just taken place. This was followed by a debriefing lunch for all, and the focus group participants were asked to write up their reflections on the meeting. The researchers in turn reflected upon and discussed the focus group. Bill and Olaison (2009: 24) describe and evaluate this indirect approach to investigating a topic using a combination of focus group and role play, and conclude that it allows researchers to address the knowledge and experience of the participants as it is manifested in everyday action rather than as it is framed in the narrations offered during for instance a normal interview. The role-play-enhanced focus group method, however, requires a lot of preparatory work when staging the session and a great deal of patience among the researchers.

Another style of focus group is the 'deliberative discussion' as proposed by Rothwell et al. (2016), in which participants are informed and educated about the topic prior to the focus group. This is thought to promote the capture of quality data from enhanced discussions. A further variation of the focus group is discussed in a book by Krueger and King (1998) where they look at the advantages of involving community members in developing and conducting focus groups. This kind of research is called different names such as participatory, collaborative and community-initiated, and Krueger and King talk about it as a continuum of volunteer participation. This continuum ranges from focus groups controlled by researchers through to those controlled by the volunteers. Another form of focus group takes place at the end or near the end of a project when the researcher has some findings they wish to share with the participants who contributed to the original data collection. This use of 'feedback focus groups' can serve two purposes. First, the promise to disseminate and discuss findings with research participants may act as an incentive to take part in the research, and thus facilitate access to an organisation or group. This is especially useful when access is anticipated to be a challenge. Second, a feedback focus group can act as a convenient and effective way to ensure dissemination of findings to populations which are outside academia and therefore have no access to, or interest in, academic publications.

SUMMARY

In Chapter 5, we have illustrated the variety of focus group design with reference to published studies, and have seen how much the focus group has to offer to both academic and practitioner research, either as a stand-alone method or as part of a multiple or mixed methods design. Each example was used to demonstrate why focus groups were chosen to investigate a specific purpose, whether that was to explore a new topic, develop theory, gather impressions, diagnose problems or illuminate results from previous data.

In the final chapter, we turn our attention to the strengths and weaknesses inherent in the focus group method and briefly outline the next steps for the researcher.

6

CONCLUSIONS

INTRODUCTION

In the earlier parts of this book we explained why focus groups are a good method for gathering qualitative data to gain in-depth insights, making use of the group dynamic. In this chapter, we conclude the book by assessing the focus group and outlining its advantages and disadvantages. We consider what makes a good focus group and then we very briefly outline the next steps for the researcher once the focus groups have been completed.

CRITIQUING FOCUS GROUPS

So far in this book we have addressed how focus groups can be used in a research project, from initial considerations of the method to the actual group moderation. In the following sections we identify the advantages and disadvantages of using focus groups in a dissertation or project, and take a step back to reflect on what it is that makes a good focus group.

Advantages of focus groups

As we suggested in Chapter 1, the focus group has established itself in the social sciences as a popular and enduring research method. Such popularity indicates that there are many published studies which document the use of focus groups, as we saw in Chapter 5, but also many resources which discuss the method in great detail, such as textbooks. This wide range of literature on focus groups provides a wealth of information and help to the researcher who is encountering the method for the first time. A second advantage of using focus groups is their flexibility. As we have covered in previous chapters, focus groups can be used on their own, within a mixed or multi-methods research inquiry, and are suitable to address a variety of research questions from different epistemological positions. The focus group can be structured in a number of ways and can be used throughout the research process, from beginning to end. A third advantage is the way that focus groups can be adapted to the digital environment, for example to be used in an online format, or in a virtual world with avatars. Such innovation means that the method is continually developing and offering exciting opportunities to the researcher.

The ability to generate multiple layers of data is a fourth advantage of focus groups, as is their suitability to incorporate different activities and techniques, some of which we illustrated in Chapters 2 and 5. A final advantage is the enjoyment of actually doing a focus group, and the skill that increases with each experience of moderation. It is a very good way to find out about something which interests you, and has the potential to provide rich and complex data.

Disadvantages of focus groups

No research method is without its disadvantages and the focus group is no exception. Having identified the advantages, we now turn to what might be seen as the negative aspects of focus groups. What will have come across in Chapters 3 and 4 is the amount of time that planning and running focus groups can take. The organisation required to recruit participants and ensure they all turn up on the right day at the right time is not a quick process. Finding participants who can commit to perhaps a two-hour focus group plus journey time is not an easy task. Once the group has been moderated, additional time is needed to transcribe and possibly translate, both of which are often more time consuming than expected. There are practical means of addressing the time issue: plan well ahead for recruitment, and allow extra time for all the necessary steps after the group has been held.

We mentioned that one of the advantages of using focus groups is the opportunity to moderate, which can be a very enjoyable and informative experience. However, to be able to moderate a focus group demands a set of skills, including the ability to manage a group of people, to encourage participation from quiet members and equally to handle dominant participants who seek to overwhelm the group. These are not skills which are usually developed elsewhere or in other situations. Thus, a disadvantage of using focus groups is that the researcher has to acquire these skills prior to collecting data. It is therefore useful to have a practice focus group with friends or peers before running the pilot group. Again, this would need to be built into the project to allow sufficient time before the main data collection.

Another disadvantage of using focus groups is the nature and amount of data that is collected. Because focus groups tend to feature a small number of participants and generate qualitative data, research which is produced with this method might be seen as less credible in business and management fields than research informed by other methods such as questionnaires and quantitative analysis. Stewart and Shamdasani (2015: 49) comment that there is an unfortunate tendency among some social scientists 'to regard focus groups as appropriate or inappropriate, sound or unsound, without regard to the research question'. This may apply to dissertation supervisors, who will have their own view on the appropriateness of various methods. The response to this point is to make sure your choice to use focus groups can be defended, and reference to the criteria for assessing the quality of research inquiry, as outlined in Chapter 2, might be helpful in this defence.

Like all research methods, focus groups have both advantages and disadvantages associated with their use. On reflection, we would suggest that the former outweigh the latter, mainly because the quality and richness of the data that focus groups provide can overcome the disadvantages identified above. Any method brings challenges and problems, especially if it is one you have never used before. The key consideration is to select the method that you feel will help you most to address your research questions.

What makes a good focus group?

Throughout this book, we have attempted to highlight what it is that makes a good focus group. We have discussed the value of being well prepared, of understanding how the choice of method relates to philosophical assumptions, and the importance of linking research method to research questions. We have also discussed practical tips on how to actually moderate a focus group. So what makes a focus group 'good'? We suggest it is the quality of group interaction which directly links to the quality of the data collected, and hence to the quality of the research project overall. If that is all just a little too vague, we can go back to the criteria for assessing the quality of research inquiry discussed in Chapter 2. By adhering to established criteria, which fit with one's epistemological position, the research can be given a clear rationale and account which make sense to the reader. We would also stress the ethical dimension of research with focus groups, with careful attention to capturing the voices of the participants in a transparent and authentic manner. In essence, the focus group will be part of a well-designed study, clearly argued and presented, and with a consistent narrative running through from start to finish.

AFTER THE FOCUS GROUP: THINKING ABOUT NEXT STEPS

In this section, we briefly discuss what comes after the focus group has finished, and what tasks remain for the researcher. We do not discuss how to do the analysis, as other books in this series address specific analysis techniques which you may find applicable to your study. For example, the book by Greatbatch and Clark (forthcoming) looks at conversation analysis, which would be one option for analysing focus group data. Any analysis strategy would link back to the different types of focus group, which we introduced in Chapter 2. For example, if the aim of the focus group was to act as a precursor to a later survey, and was intent on documenting objective facts, then a quantitative content analysis would be a potential way of analysing the data. A narrative analysis approach would be more appropriate for focus groups carried out from an interpretive position. There are many forms of analysis open to the researcher, and one key consideration is personal preference. Some researchers feel more comfortable with a particular technique, and this preference will likely have been evident in the initial choice of focus group design. Thus, analysis will be linked to earlier considerations of the underlying philosophical assumptions of the research.

The second point we would like to make about data analysis and focus groups is to point to the level of analysis. Because of the importance of the interactive nature of the data (i.e. the discussions between the participants), data analysis needs to be conducted at different levels. This implies analysis at both the individual level and the group level.

CONCLUSIONS

In this book we have provided an overview of the focus group method as might be used in projects and dissertations by business and management researchers. We have addressed the different forms that focus groups can take; the issues to be considered before focus groups are chosen; how focus groups can be planned, organised and moderated; challenges to be overcome; and what happens once the focus groups are finished.

Conducting focus groups can be a very rewarding experience for researchers as focus groups have the capacity to generate rich and interesting data. We hope that we have shed some light on the process of using focus groups for your dissertations and projects.

REFERENCES

Abrams, K.M., Wang, Z., Song, Y.J. and Galindo-Gonzalez, S. (2015) 'Data richness trade-offs between face-to-face, online audiovisual, and online text-only focus groups'. *Social Science Computer Review*, 33 (1): 80–96.

Ahrens, T. (2004) 'Refining research questions in the course of negotiating access for fieldwork', in C. Humphrey and B. Lee. (eds), *The Real Life Guide to Accounting Research: A behind-the-scenes view of using qualitative research methods*. Oxford: Elsevier (pp. 295–308).

Alevizou, P.J., Oates, C.J. and McDonald, S. (2015) 'The well(s) of knowledge: The decoding of sustainability claims in the UK and in Greece'. *Sustainability*, 7: 8729–47.

Allen, M.D. (2014) 'Telephone focus groups: Strengths, challenges, and strategies for success'. *Qualitative Social Work*, 13 (4): 571–83.

Barbour, R. (2007) *Doing Focus Groups*. London: Sage.

Barbour, R. (2014) 'Analysing focus groups', in U. Flick (ed.), *The SAGE Handbook of Qualitative Data Analysis*. London: Sage (pp. 313–26).

Barbour, R. and Kitzinger, J. (eds) (1998) *Developing Focus Group Research: Politics, theory and practice*. London: Sage.

Basch, C. (1987) 'Focus group interview: an underutilized research technique for improving theory and practice in health education'. *Health Education Quarterly*, 14: 411–48.

Bernon, M. and Cullen, J. (2007) 'An integrated approach to managing reverse logistics'. *International Journal of Logistics Research and Applications*, 10 (1): 41–56.

Bill, F. and Olaison, L. (2009) 'The indirect approach of semi-focused groups: Expanding focus group research through role-playing'. *Qualitative Research in Organizations and Management: An International Journal*, 4 (1): 7-26.

Bloor, M., Frankland, J., Thomas, M. and Robson, K. (2001) *Focus Groups in Social Research*. London: Sage.

Brici, N., Hodkinson, C. and Sullivan-Mort, G. (2013) 'Conceptual differences between adolescent and adult impulse buyers'. *Young Consumers*, 14 (3): 258–79.

Brislin, R.W. (1970) 'Back-translation for cross-cultural research'. *Journal of Cross-Cultural Psychology*, 1 (3): 185–216.

Brondani, M.A., MacEntee, M.I., Bryant, S.R. and O'Neill, B. (2008) 'Using written vignettes in focus groups among older adults to discuss oral health as a sensitive topic'. *Qualitative Health Research*, 18 (8): 1145–53.

Brüggen, E. and Willems, P. (2009) 'A critical comparison of offline focus groups, online focus groups and e-Delphi'. *International Journal of Market Research*, 51 (3): 363–81.

Bryman, A. (2016) *Social Research Methods*. Oxford: Oxford University Press.

Buckingham, D. (1987) *Public Secrets: EastEnders and its Audience*. London: British Film Institute.

Carey, M.A. (1994) 'The group effect in focus groups: Planning, implementing, and interpreting focus group research', in J.M. Morse (ed.), *Critical Issues in Qualitative Research Methods*. Thousand Oaks, CA: Sage (pp. 225–41).

Carey, M.A. and Smith, M.W. (1992) 'Enhancement of validity through qualitative approaches incorporating the patient's perspective'. *Evaluation and the Health Professions*, 15 (1): 107–14.

Cassell, C. (2015) *Conducting Research Interviews for Business and Management Students*. London: Sage.

Chan, K., Ng, Y.L. and Luk, E.K. (2013) 'Impact of celebrity endorsement in advertising on brand image among Chinese adolescents'. *Young Consumers*, 14 (2): 167–79.

Chong, E., Alayli-Goebbels, A., Webel-Edgar, L., Muir, S. and Manson, H. (2015) 'Advancing telephone focus groups method through the use of webinar methodological reflections on evaluating Ontario, Canada's healthy babies healthy children program'. *Global Qualitative Nursing Research*, 2: 1–8.

Cochoy, F. (2015) 'Consumers at work, or curiousity at play? Revisiting the presumption/value cocreation debate with smartphones and two-dimensional bar codes'. *Marketing Theory*, 15 (2): 133–53.

Colucci, E. (2007) '"Focus groups can be fun": The use of activity-oriented questions in focus group discussions'. *Qualitative Health Research*, 17 (10): 1422–33.

Coule, T. (2013) 'Theories of knowledge and focus groups in organization and management research'. *Qualitative Research in Organizations and Management: An International Journal*, 8 (2): 148–62.

Crowley, G.H., Leffel, R., Ramirez, D., Hart, J.L. and Armstrong, T.S. (2002) 'Users' perceptions of the library's web pages: A focus group study at Texas A and M University'. *The Journal of Academic Librarianship*, 28 (4): 205–10.

Culley, L., Hudson, N. and Rapport, F. (2007) 'Using focus groups with minority ethnic communities: Researching infertility in British South Asian communities'. *Qualitative Health Research*, 17 (1): 102–12.

Daymon, C. and Holloway, I. (2011) *Qualitative Research Methods in Public Relations and Marketing Communications*. London: Routledge.

Deggs, D., Grover, K. and Kacirek, K. (2010) 'Expectations of adult graduate students in an online degree program'. *College Student Journal*, 44 (3): 690.

Easterby-Smith, M., Thorpe, R. and Jackson, P.R. (2015) *Management and Business Research,* 5th edition. London: Sage.

Esposito, N. (2001) 'From meaning to meaning: The influence of translation techniques on non-English focus group research'. *Qualitative Health Research,* 11 (4): 568-79.

Finch, H. and Lewis, J. (2003) 'Focus groups'. In H. Finch and J. Lewis (eds), *Qualitative Research Practice: A guide for social science students and researchers.* Thousand Oaks, CA: Sage (pp. 170-98).

Flick, U. (2014) *An Introduction to Qualitative Research,* 5th edition. Los Angeles: Sage.

Gadalla, E., Abosag, I. and Keeling, K. (2016) 'Second Life as a research environment: Avatar-based focus groups (AFG)'. *Qualitative Market Research: An International Journal,* 19 (1): 101-14.

Gentina, E. and Singh, P. (2015) 'How national culture and parental style affect the process of adolescents' ecological resocialization'. *Sustainability,* 7: 7581-603.

Ghauri, P. and Grønhaug, K. (2005) *Research Methods in Business Studies,* 3rd edition. Harlow: Pearson.

Gothberg, J., Applegate, B., Reeves, P., Kohler, P., Thurston, L. and Peterson, L. (2013) 'Is the medium really the message? A comparison of face-to-face, telephone, and internet focus group venues'. *Journal of Ethnographic and Qualitative Research,* 7: 108-27.

Greatbatch, D. and Clark, T. (forthcoming) *Using Conversation Analysis for Business and Management Students.* London: Sage.

Greenbaum, T.L. (2000) *Moderating Focus Groups: A practical guide for group facilitation.* Thousand Oaks, CA: Sage.

Harrison, R.L. (2013) 'Using mixed methods designs in the Journal of Business Research', 1990-2010. *Journal of Business Research,* 66: 2153-62.

Herington, C., Scott, D. and Johnson, L.W. (2005) 'Focus group exploration of firm-employee relationship strength'. *Qualitative Market Research: An International Journal,* 8 (3): 256-76.

Holzwarth, M., Janiszewski, C. and Neumann, M.M. (2006) 'The influence of avatars on online consumer shopping behaviour'. *Journal of Marketing,* 70 (4): 19-36.

Horta, A., Truninger, M., Alexandre, S., Teixeira, J. and Aparecida da Silva, V. (2013) 'Children's food meanings and eating contexts: Schools and their surroundings'. *Young Consumers,* 14 (4): 312-20.

Hurworth, R. (2005) 'The use of telephone focus groups for qualitative research'. *Qualitative Research Journal,* 5 (1): 90.

Jagosh, J. and Boudreau, J.D. (2009) 'Lost and found in translation: An ecological approach to bilingual research methodology'. *International Journal of Qualitative Methods,* 8 (2): 102-114.

Johnson, P., Buehring, A., Cassell, C. and Symon, G. (2006) 'Evaluating qualitative management research: Towards a contingent criteriology'. *International Journal of Management Reviews,* 8 (3): 131-56.

Joseph, D.H., Griffin, M. and Sullivan, E.D. (2000) 'Videotaped focus groups: Transforming a therapeutic strategy into a research tool'. *Nursing Forum,* 35 (1): 15.

Kinnear, T.C. and Taylor, J.R. (1996) *Marketing Research: An applied orientation*. New York: McGraw-Hill.

Kitzinger, J. (1994) 'The methodology of focus groups: The importance of interaction between research participants'. *Sociology of Health and Illness*, 16 (1): 103–21.

Knittel, Z., Beurer, K. and Berndt, A. (2016) 'Brand avoidance among Generation Y consumers'. *Qualitative Market Research: An International Journal*, 19 (1): 27–43.

Krueger, R.A. (1994) *Focus Groups: A Practical Guide for Applied Research*, 2nd edition. Thousand Oaks, CA: Sage.

Krueger, R.A. (1998) 'Developing questions for focus groups'. In D.L. Morgan, R.A. Krueger and J.A. King (eds) *Focus Group Kit*, Vol. 3. Thousand Oaks, CA: Sage.

Krueger, R.A. and Casey, M.A. (2015) *Focus Groups: A practical guide for applied research*, 5th edition. Thousand Oaks, CA: Sage.

Krueger, R.A. and King, J.A. (1998) *Involving Community Members in Focus Groups*. Thousand Oaks, CA: Sage.

Langford, J. and McDonagh, D. (2003) *Focus Groups: Supporting effective product development*. London: Taylor & Francis.

Larkin, P.J., de Casterlé, B.D. and Schotsmans, P. (2007) 'Multilingual translation issues in qualitative research reflections on a metaphorical process'. *Qualitative Health Research*, 17 (4): 468–76.

Liamputtong, P. (2011) *Focus Group Methodology: Principles and practice*. Los Angeles: Sage.

Lunt, P. and Livingstone, S. (1996) 'Rethinking the focus group in media and communication research'. *Journal of Communication*, 46 (2): 79–98.

MacDougall, C. and Fudge, E. (2001) 'Planning and recruiting the sample for focus groups and in-depth interviews'. *Qualitative Health Research*, 11 (1): 117–26.

MacNaghten, P. and Myers, G. (2004) 'Focus groups', in C. Seale, G. Gobo, J. Gubrium and D. Silverman (eds), *Qualitative Research Practice*. London: Sage (pp. 65–80).

Malhotra, N.K. (2010) *Marketing Research: An applied orientation*, 6th edition. New Jersey: Pearson.

McDermott, M.J. (2013) 'Take your pick'. *Association of National Advertisers Magazine*, Spring: 32–42.

Merton, R.K., Fiske, M. and Kendall, P.L. (1956) *The Focused Interview: A manual of problems and procedures*. Glencoe, IL: The Free Press.

Miles, M.B., Huberman, A.M. and Saldana, J. (2014) *Qualitative Data Analysis: A methods sourcebook*, 3rd edition. Thousand Oaks, CA: Sage.

Morgan, D.L. (1988) *Focus Groups as Qualitative Research*. Newbury Park, CA: Sage.

Morgan, D.L. (1996) 'Focus groups'. *Annual Review of Sociology*, 22: 129–52.

Morgan, D.L. (1997) *Focus Groups as Qualitative Research*, 2nd edition. Thousand Oaks, CA: Sage.

Morgan, D.L. (1998) *The Focus Group Guidebook: Focus Group Kit 1*. Thousand Oaks, CA: Sage.

Morgan, D.L. and Krueger, R.A. (1993) 'When to use focus groups and why', in D.L. Morgan (ed.), *Successful Focus Groups: Advancing the state of the art*. Newbury Park, CA: Sage (pp. 3-19).

Morgan, D.L. with Scannell, A.U. (1998) *Planning Focus Groups: Focus group kit 2*. Thousand Oaks, CA: Sage.

Moses, J.W. and Knutsen, T.L. (2012) *Ways of Knowing: Competing methodologies in social and political research*, 2nd edition. Basingstoke: Palgrave.

Newman, N. and Oates, C.J. (2014) 'Parental mediation of food marketing communications aimed at children'. *International Journal of Advertising*, 33 (3): 579-98.

Nicholas, D.B., Lach, L., King, G., Scott, M., Boydell, K., Sawatzky, B.J., Reisman, J., Schippel, E. and Young, N.L. (2010) 'Contrasting Internet and face-to-face focus groups for children with chronic health conditions: Outcomes and participant experiences'. *International Journal of Qualitative Methods*, 9 (1): 105-21.

Nurkka, P., Kujala, S. and Kemppainen, K. (2009) 'Capturing users' perceptions of valuable experience and meaning'. *Journal of Engineering Design*, 20 (5): 449-65.

Oates, C.J. (2000) 'Gift giving, reciprocity and women's weekly magazines'. *Self, Agency and Society*, 3 (1): 70-97.

Oates, C.J., Blades, M., Gunter, B. and Don, J. (2003) 'Children's understanding of television advertising: A qualitative approach'. *Journal of Marketing Communications*, 9 (2): 59-72.

Osborn, A.F. (1957) *Applied Imagination* revised edition. New York: Scribner.

Oxford Dictionary (2016) 'Definition of post-16 in English'. Available at: www.oxford dictionaries.com/definition/english/generation-y (last accessed 7 June 2017).

Patton, M.Q. (2015) *Qualitative Research and Evaluation Methods*. Thousand Oaks, CA: Sage.

Peattie, K., Peattie, S. and Clarke, P. (2001) 'Skin cancer prevention: Re-evaluating the public policy implications'. *Journal of Public Policy and Marketing*, 20 (2): 268-79.

Pendry, L.F., Mewse, A.J. and Burgoyne, C.B. (2012) 'Environmentally friendly parenting: Are cloth nappies a step too far?' *Young Consumers*, 13 (1): 5-19.

Pettigrew, S. and Charters, S. (2008) 'Tasting as a projective technique'. *Qualitative Market Research: An International Journal*, 11 (3): 331-43.

Pich, C. and Dean, D. (2015) 'Qualitative projective techniques in political brand image research from the perspective of young adults'. *Qualitative Market Research: An International Journal*, 18 (1): 115-44.

Poland, B.D. (1995) 'Transcription quality as an aspect of rigor in qualitative research'. *Qualitative Inquiry*, 1 (3): 290-310.

Rodrigues, V.S., Piecyk, M., Potter, A., McKinnon, A., Naim, M. and Edwards, J. (2010) 'Assessing the application of focus groups as a method for collecting data in logistics'. *International Journal of Logistics Research and Applications*, 13 (1): 75-94.

Rothwell, E., Anderson, R. and Botkin, J.R. (2016) 'Deliberative discussion focus groups'. *Qualitative Health Research*, 26 (6): 734-40.

Saunders, M., Lewis, P. and Thornhill, A. (2016) *Research Methods for Business Students*, 7th edition. Harlow: Pearson.

Scholl, N., Mulders, S. and Drent, R. (2002) 'On-line qualitative market research: Interviewing the world at a fingertip'. *Qualitative Market Research: An International Journal*, 5 (3): 210–23.

Shammas, D. (2017) 'Underreporting discrimination among Arab American and Muslim American community college students: Using focus groups to unravel the ambiguities within the survey data'. *Journal of Mixed Methods Research*, 11 (1): 99–123.

Silver, C. and Lewins, A. (2014) *Using Software in Qualitative Research: A step-by-step guide*, 2nd edition. Los Angeles: Sage.

Smith, J.M., Sullivan, J.S. and Baxter, D.G. (2009) 'Telephone focus groups in physiotherapy research: Potential uses and recommendations'. *Physiotherapy Theory and Practice*, 25 (4): 241–56.

Smith, M.W. (1995) 'Ethics in focus groups: A few concerns'. *Qualitative Health Research*, 5: 478–86.

Sohail, M.S. and Shaikh, N.M. (2004) 'Quest for excellence in business education: A study of student impressions of service quality'. *International Journal of Educational Management*, 18 (1): 58–65.

Spanjaard, D., Young, L. and Freeman, L. (2014) 'Emotions in supermarket brand choice'. *Qualitative Market Research: An International Journal*, 17 (3): 209–24.

Squires, A. (2009) 'Methodological challenges in cross-language qualitative research: A research review'. *International Journal of Nursing Studies*, 46 (2): 277–87.

Stewart, D.W. and Shamdasani, P.N. (2015) *Focus Groups: Theory and practice*. Newbury Park, CA: Sage.

Steyaert, C. and Bouwen, R. (2004) 'Group methods of organizational analysis', in C. Cassell and G. Symon (eds), *Essential Guide to Qualitative Methods in Organizational Research*. London: Sage (pp. 140–53).

Stiles, D.R. (2004) 'Pictorial representation', in C. Cassell and G. Symon (eds), *Essential Guide to Qualitative Methods in Organizational Research*. London: Sage (pp. 127–39).

Sweet, C. (2001) 'Designing and conducting virtual focus groups'. *Qualitative Market Research: An International Journal*, 4 (3): 130–35.

Temple, B. and Young, A. (2004) 'Qualitative research and translation dilemmas'. *Qualitative Research*, 4 (2): 161–78.

Tinson, J. (2009) *Conducting Research with Children and Adolescents*. Oxford: Goodfellow Publishers.

Tuckman, B.W. (1964) 'Personality structure, group composition, and group functioning'. *Sociometry*, 27 (4): 469–87.

Tuttas, C.A. (2015) 'Lessons learned using web conference technology for online focus group interviews'. *Qualitative Health Research*, 25 (1): 122–33.

Woodyatt, C.R., Finneran, C.A. and Stephenson, R. (2016) 'In-person versus online focus group discussions: A comparative analysis of data quality'. *Qualitative Health Research*, 26 (6): 741–49.

INDEX